# Endorsements

"The pursuit of a regimented godliness is not unique to Christianity, but it is rare. Unlike popular versions of the Christian faith, Jonathan Edwards did not seek the disciplines of godliness for utilitarian ends, the self-help preoccupation of Western Christianity. He saw conformity to Christ as a means, the only means, to glorify God. Steve Lawson has done a wonderful service, producing in a tactful and pastoral manner Edwards' pious resolutions, thereby helping us understand the inner life, the spiritual struggles and goals, of perhaps America's greatest intellect."

—DR. JOHN D. HANNAH
Research professor of theological studies
and distinguished professor of historical theology,
Dallas Theological Seminary

"Tired of going at the Christian life in piecemeal fashion? Tired of half-hearted pursuits? Then you've come to the right book. Here Steven Lawson artfully points you to Jonathan Edwards, a model for pursuing holiness, humility, and love, and for the forsaking of sin—all driven by a relentless passion 'to glorify God and enjoy him forever.' When Edwards wrote his 'Resolutions,' he likely had no idea how much they would impact his life. Beware, they'll do the same for you."

—DR. STEPHEN J. NICHOLS
Research professor of Christianity and culture,
Lancaster Bible College

"The growing embrace of Reformed thought in the past quarter of a century has been very encouraging to those of us who delight in this most biblical expression of Christianity. And the remarkable writings of Jonathan Edwards have, by the grace of God, played no little part in this expansion of Reformed theology. This new volume by Steve Lawson helps to locate the root of Edwards' thinking in his close walk with God. It serves as a powerful reminder that Reformed orthodoxy and Reformed piety belong together, and that to focus on the former at the expense of the latter is not only un-Edwardsean, but also un-biblical."

—DR. MICHAEL A. G. HAYKIN
Professor of church history and biblical spirituality,
The Southern Baptist Theological Seminary

The Unwavering Resolve of

# Jonathan
# Edwards

A **Long Line of Godly Men** Profile

The Unwavering Resolve of

# Jonathan Edwards

STEVEN J. LAWSON

**R** *Reformation Trust*   A DIVISION OF LIGONIER MINISTRIES, ORLANDO, FL

*The Unwavering Resolve of Jonathan Edwards*

© 2008 by Steven J. Lawson

Published by Reformation Trust Publishing
a division of Ligonier Ministries
421 Ligonier Court, Sanford, FL 32771
Ligonier.org    ReformationTrust.com

Printed in Crawfordsville, Indiana
RR Donnelley and Sons
June 2014
First edition, fourth printing

Cover design: Chris Larson
Cover illustration: Kent Barton
Interior design and typeset: Katherine Lloyd, The DESK

The text of Jonathan Edwards' "Resolutions" in the appendix is reprinted
from *The Works of Jonathan Edwards, Vol. 16, Letters and Personal Writings*, ed. George S. Claghorn (New Haven, Conn.: Yale University Press,
1998), 753–759. © 1998 by Yale University. All rights reserved. Used by permission. All citations of particular resolutions are from the same source.

All Scripture quotations are from *The Holy Bible, English Standard Version*,
copyright © 2001 by Crossway Bibles, a division of Good News Publishers.
Used by permission. All rights reserved.

**Library of Congress Cataloging-in-Publication Data**

Lawson, Steven J.
  The unwavering resolve of Jonathan Edwards / Steven J. Lawson.
     p. cm.
  ISBN 978-1-56769-108-5
  1. Edwards, Jonathan, 1703-1758.  I. Title.
  BX7260.E3L35 2008
  285.8092--dc22
  [B]

                                2008030951

This book is dedicated to the two lead elders with whom I serve at Christ Fellowship Baptist Church in Mobile, Alabama:

*Tom Gibson*
and
*Danny Chance*

These faithful men have stood by my side since God first planted the church we are now privileged to serve and oversee. Like Jonathan Edwards, they are marked by unwavering resolve in their pursuit of personal holiness and in their shepherding of the flock of God. Heaven one day will reveal their fixed determination to do God's work God's way for God's glory. Until then, may you know of their diligent ministry.

*Therefore, my beloved brethren, be steadfast, immovable, always abounding in the work of the Lord, knowing that your toil is not in vain in the Lord.*

(1 COR. 15:58, NASB)

# Contents

# The Pursuit of Holiness

L iving the Christian life, by all biblical accounts, necessitates the passionate pursuit of personal holiness. Sanctification is never an elective course that a believer may or may not take. Neither is it an upper-level graduate study, required for only a few disciples. Instead, it is a core class, mandated for all Christians. Godliness is a lifelong study, for no one graduates from the school of Christ this side of heaven.

Progress in personal holiness is absolutely crucial. The Bible says, "Pursue . . . sanctification without which no one will see the Lord" (Heb. 12:14, NASB). In other words, the path that leads to heaven must lead first to holiness. Jesus said, "Blessed are the pure in heart, for they shall see God" (Matt. 5:8). Growth in godliness marks *all* who are on the narrow path that leads to life.

To be sure, this pursuit necessitates self-discipline. The

apostle Paul wrote, "I discipline my body and make it my slave, so that, after I have preached to others, I myself will not be disqualified" (1 Cor. 9:27, NASB). In the ancient games, an athlete who failed to meet basic training requirements could not participate at all, much less win the crown. In the same way, the believer who fails to buffet his body and bring it into submission is put out of the race. If one fails to exercise self-control, he forfeits the prize.

The apostle is not saying that such an undisciplined believer will lose his salvation, for such is impossible. Scripture clearly affirms the eternal security of the believer. Rather, the undisciplined disciple loses personal joy, spiritual power, and, ultimately, eternal reward (1 Cor. 3:15). To win the prize, all believers must "lay aside every encumbrance and the sin which so easily entangles us . . . [and] run with endurance the race that is set before us" (Heb. 12:1, NASB). Simply put, "No pain, no gain."

Paul reinforces this challenge with these words: "Discipline yourself for the purpose of godliness" (1 Tim. 4:7, NASB). By this exhortation, Paul called for the kind of strict training that a champion athlete undergoes in order to gain the crown. In the Christian life, rigorous discipline, motivated and enabled by grace, is required of all on the path to victory. Spiritual sluggards, beware!

In light of these biblical teachings, it is astounding how many professing believers are slack regarding the self-discipline needed for growth in godliness. We live in a day of spiritual laxity. Many who confess Christ are pampering themselves to death rather than pushing themselves to holiness. Their spiritual muscles are untrained and unfit. Their wills are soft and unresolved.

This is why a study of the life of Jonathan Edwards is so valuable. Considered *the* towering figure in American Colonial church history—arguably the greatest pastor, preacher, philosopher, theologian, and author America has ever produced—Edwards lived with an enlarged desire to experience personal godliness. In this pursuit, he became a model of discipline worthy of our emulation.

As an eighteen- and nineteen-year-old man, in 1722 and 1723, Edwards wrote seventy purpose statements for his life, known as his "Resolutions." Although he had been a Christian for only a year, Edwards knew that he must discipline himself for daily growth in holiness. As a result, with steely determination, this young Puritan minister wrote and worked hard to keep these seventy vows. Here is the key to his spiritual growth—Edwards disciplined himself for the purpose of godliness. He understood that growth in holiness is not a one-time act, but a lifelong pursuit, one that requires a daily determination to live according to the truths taught in Scripture. In accordance with his "Resolutions," Edwards consecrated himself in all things in order to glorify God and gain the incorruptible crown.

This book is the second in a series titled *The Long Line of Godly Men Profiles*. In the first volume, *The Expository Genius of John Calvin*, we examined the preaching ministry of the great

Genevan Reformer of the sixteenth century, who so masterfully expounded the Scriptures. In this volume, we will consider the personal piety of Edwards, who lived in eighteenth-century America. This New England divine pursued an authentic spirituality that distinguished him as a man of God. Future volumes will focus on Martin Luther, George Whitefield, Charles Spurgeon, and others, noting their far-reaching influence upon church history. Much spiritual profit is to be gained from studying the personal lives and public ministries of these spiritual leaders.

As we focus on Edwards, we will discover that he prized personal purity because he so treasured the splendor of God's holiness. "The beauty of Christianity is the beauty of holiness," David Vaughan writes. "And the enduring attraction of Edwards' life and teaching is not his metaphysical subtlety, not his keen intellect, but rather the beauty of his personal holiness."[1] Therefore, our emphasis in this volume will be Edwards' passionate pursuit of personal godliness through his "Resolutions." Space will not permit us to consider every resolution, but we shall study a great many of them in various categories. For further reflection, the complete text of the "Resolutions" can be found in an appendix at the end of this book.

The ultimate goal of this book is to challenge a new generation of believers to pursue holiness in their daily lives. My aim is to fix our sights on how we must be disciplined in this pursuit. To sharpen our focus, we will supplement our consideration of individual resolutions with passages from Edwards' diary and his "Personal Narrative" in order to gain insights into how he implemented them. By so doing, we will observe a model of a disciplined Christian life.

If you are a believer, may the unwavering resolve of Jonathan Edwards challenge you to live with a higher degree of commitment in your spiritual life. If you are not yet a believer, may his life reveal what a true Christian looks like and cause you to trust and follow Christ.

I want to thank the publishing team at Reformation Trust for their commitment to this series of profiles. Once again, I want to express my gratitude to Greg Bailey, director of publications, who has done an excellent job editing this manuscript and encouraging me. Also, Chris Larson, director of communications, was instrumental in the beautiful graphic design of this book. I remain proud of my association with Dr. R. C. Sproul and Ligonier Ministries.

At Christ Fellowship Baptist Church, which I have the honor to serve as senior pastor, I want to thank the elders and the congregation for supporting me in writing this book. These chapters were presented to the church as a series of messages on Wednesday evenings; I trust they were to the people's edification. I want to express my gratitude to my executive assistant, Kay Allen, who typed this document and coordinated the effort. I also owe a special debt to my eldest son, Andrew, who helped in the initial researching and editing of this book, and to Mark Hassler, who provided additional research and editorial assistance.

My family remains a tower of encouragement to me in my personal life and ministry. My wife, Anne, and our four children, Andrew, James, Grace Anne, and John, stand as one with me in this book. What I write, they believe and live.

*Soli Deo Gloria.*

—Steven J. Lawson
Mobile, Alabama
July 2008

## Note

1. David Vaughn, *A Divine Light: The Spiritual Leadership of Jonathan Edwards* (Nashville: Cumberland House, 2007), 156.

# CHAPTER ONE

# Edwards' Life and Legacy

*I am tempted, perhaps foolish, to compare the Puritans to the Alps, Luther and Calvin to the Himalayas, and Jonathan Edwards to Mount Everest! He has always seemed to me the man most like the Apostle Paul.*[1]

—D. MARTYN LLOYD-JONES

I t has been almost three centuries since Jonathan Edwards last ministered in Colonial New England, and yet, he is still widely regarded as the most distinguished minister ever to grace the American church. With enduring influence, Edwards continues to tower over the intellectual and spiritual life of the evangelical church. His theological writings were stunningly brilliant, his pastoral ministry was fruitful, and his Christian walk was exemplary.

Providentially placed into the eighteenth century, in the

1

years before the United States came into being, Edwards lived at a strategic crossroad of church history. Considered "the last of the medieval Scholastic theologians"[2] and "the last representative of Puritan theology and thought in the New World,"[3] Edwards also was "the first of the modern American philosopher-theologians."[4] In like manner, George Marsden, author of an acclaimed biography of Edwards, calls him "the most acute early American philosopher."[5] Revered Princeton theologian Benjamin B. Warfield agrees, asserting that Edwards "stands out as the one figure of real greatness in the intellectual life of colonial America."[6] And B. K. Kuiper writes that he was "the outstanding intellectual figure in colonial America."[7]

Many regard Edwards as the most eminent preacher ever to come from what is now the United States. He delivered what many believe to be America's most famous sermon, "Sinners in the Hands of an Angry God." Others esteem Edwards as one of America's greatest theologians. He is recognized as "the theologian of the First Great Awakening,"[8] for he stood squarely at "the headwaters of the revivals"[9] in the 1730s and 1740s. It also has been said that Edwards was America's "greatest [theologian] of any variety"[10] and one of "the half-dozen greatest theologians of all time."[11]

Edwards also excelled as a writer. Marsden believes that three of Edwards' many works—*Religious Affections, Freedom of the Will,* and *The Nature of True Virtue*—stand as "masterpieces in the larger history of Christian literature."[12] Reformed theologian R. C. Sproul estimates that *Freedom of the Will* "is the most important theological work ever published in America."[13] Paul Ramsey, an Edwardian scholar, writes that *Freedom of the Will* "is sufficient to establish its author as the greatest philosopher-theologian yet to grace the American scene."[14]

Edwards' lasting influence can be measured in other ways, as well. At the beginning of the twentieth century, a study traced Edwards' descendants. The results were staggering. From Edwards came a large and distinguished progeny: three hundred clergymen, missionaries, and theological professors; 120 college professors; 110 lawyers; more than sixty physicians; more than sixty authors of good books; thirty judges; fourteen presidents of universities; numerous giants in American industry; eighty holders of major public office; three mayors of large cities; three governors of states; three U.S. senators; one chaplain of the U.S. Senate; one comptroller of the U.S. Treasury; and one vice president of the United States.[15] It is hard to imagine that anyone else has contributed more vitally to the soul of this nation than this New England divine.

There is no doubt that Edwards was a giant of the Christian faith, one whose influence is still keenly felt today. As S. M. Houghton writes, Edwards became "a star of the first magnitude in the annals of the Church of God."[16] Meic Pearse believes that he was "the most influential single figure in American Christianity until the twentieth century—and arguably down to the present."[17] Harry S. Stout marvels over Edwards' "enduring ability to speak across the ages."[18]

## Why Jonathan Edwards?

From these facts and accolades, it is obvious that Edwards' life is worthy of our study and emulation. But certain questions beg to be addressed: What made Edwards so great? What caused this man to be used so effectively by God? In short, why Edwards? Ultimately, God by His sovereign grace chose Edwards to be a distinguished and influential leader. But on a more personal and practical level, Edwards uniquely combined spiritual godliness with intellectual genius. Both his mind and his heart were engaged in the pursuit of God, his piety the equal of his intellect. D. Martyn Lloyd-Jones believed this was the key to Edwards' achievements: "The spiritual always controlled the intellectual in him."[19] In other words, "All his rich and brilliant gifts were not only held to be subservient, but were used as servants."[20] To put it yet another way, Lloyd-Jones writes, Edwards was "God-dominated."[21]

In short, though Edwards was intellectually brilliant and theologically commanding, his true greatness lay in his indefatigable zeal for the glory of God. He was distinguished as a man after God's own heart by his "profound . . . and exceptional spirituality."[22] The soul of this American Puritan was devoted to pursuing the unrivaled honor of God. In a word, Edwards was *resolved*. He was determined to live with uncompromising fidelity for the greatness of God. His eye was singular; his soul was steadfast; his will was strong. This fixed determination to seek the majesty of God will be the focus of this book.

Let us begin our study of Jonathan Edwards with a survey of his remarkable life.

## A Puritan in the Making (1703–1726)

Born Oct. 5, 1703, to the Rev. Timothy and Esther Stoddard Edwards in East Windsor, Connecticut, Jonathan Edwards was the only son among ten daughters. His was one of the most respected families of Colonial America. Edwards' father was a Harvard-trained pastor who faithfully preached at the same church in East Windsor for more than sixty years (1694–1758). His mother came from one of the most prominent families in Connecticut, perhaps in all New England. She was the daughter of Solomon Stoddard, who pastored one church for almost sixty years (1672–1729), the congregation in Northampton, Massachusetts, one of the most prestigious flocks in the early Colonies. Such was Stoddard's stature that he was known as "the Northampton Pope" and the "Pope of the Connecticut River Valley."[23]

Remarkable brilliance marked Jonathan as a young man. His father, an "excellent teacher [and] . . . strict disciplinarian,"[24] taught him, along with many of the town's children, giving him a superior grammar and secondary education. Timothy groomed young Jonathan for the ministry by teaching him the Scriptures, the Westminster Shorter Catechism, and Reformed theology. From his father, he also received first-hand exposure to the Christian life and the responsibilities and rewards of pastoral ministry. His mother, Esther, was known for her "native intelligence . . . [and also was] demanding."[25] Jonathan's ten sisters all were sent to Boston for finishing school and, upon returning home, assisted their brother in his studies. As a result of these influences, young Edwards was well-focused upon God and the richness of Puritan theology. Nevertheless, Jonathan was not converted to Christ during these formative years.

When Jonathan was thirteen, Timothy enrolled him at the newly founded Collegiate School of Connecticut, later to be known as Yale College. Timothy had been educated at Harvard, which had been established as a Calvinistic school, but had weakened under Arminian influences. This doctrinal erosion prompted Timothy to enroll Jonathan at Yale, which was unashamedly true to Reformed theology. In the bachelor's program, Edwards received a broad liberal-arts education, studying grammar, rhetoric, logic, ancient history, arithmetic, geometry, astronomy, metaphysics, ethics, natural science, Greek, Hebrew, Christian theology, natural philosophy, and classical literature. He also received a healthy exposure to the greatest Puritan and Reformed minds, reading John Calvin, John Owen, William Ames, and other divines. He graduated at the head of his class with a bachelor of arts degree in 1720 and delivered the valedictory address.

Edwards immediately began the master's program at Yale, which required two years of independent study. During his second year, Edwards, age seventeen, was suddenly converted to Jesus Christ. He wrote that, while he was contemplating 1 Timothy 1:17, "There came into my soul, and was as it were diffused through it, a sense of the glory of the Divine Being; a new sense, quite different from anything I ever experienced before."[26] His heart immediately was overjoyed with rapturous thoughts of God. Edwards would later write:

> I began to have a new kind of apprehensions and ideas of Christ, and the work of redemption, and the glorious ways of salvation by Him. An inward, sweet sense of these things, at times, came into my heart; and my soul was led away in pleasant views and contemplations of them. And my mind was greatly engaged to spend my time in reading and meditating on Christ, on the beauty and excellency of His person, and the lovely way of salvation by free grace in Him.[27]

Upon completing his class work for the master's program, but before writing his thesis, Edwards traveled to New York City to serve as the interim pastor of a small Scottish Presbyterian church near Broadway and Wall Street. During this formative time, he "felt a burning desire to be in everything a complete Christian."[28] This proved to be a soul-stretching time in which Edwards gave careful thought to the priorities that he desired to be the guiding principles for his life. It was then that Edwards, eighteen years old, began writing his "Resolutions." He eventually composed seventy purpose statements, each designed to direct his newly begun Christian journey. They were "the guidelines, the system of checks and balances he would use to chart out his life—his relationships, his conversations, his desires, his activities."[29] At this time, Edwards also began keeping a diary to monitor his spiritual pulse (1722–25, 1734–35). Further, Jonathan began writing his "Miscellanies," a collection of maxims, observations, and reflections, ranging from philosophical thoughts to exegetical insights into a biblical text. Wherever he was, Jonathan recorded his penetrating thoughts as they flowed from his mind, often pinning them to his coat.

When his interim pastorate concluded in April 1723, Edwards returned home to Connecticut to write his master's thesis and provide pulpit supply. He graduated from Yale in October 1723 with a master of arts degree after orally presenting and defending his thesis on the doctrine of imputation. The title of his thesis was "A Sinner is Not Justified in the Sight of God Except Through the Righteousness of Christ Obtained by Faith." Edwards then served a short interim pastorate at the Congregational church in Bolton, Connecticut, from November 1723 to May 1724, before returning to Yale to assume an instructor's position (1724–1726). It was then that he began courting young Sarah Pierpont, the daughter of James Pierpont Sr., a pastor in New Haven. The two would marry in July 1728 after a four-year courtship.

During this time, Edwards wrestled intensely with his vocational calling. Should he pursue the world of academics or the pastorate? After much soul-searching, Edwards gave himself to the high calling he had closely witnessed his father and grandfather pursue.

## EARLY YEARS AT NORTHAMPTON (1727–1739)

Young and energetic, Edwards accepted a call to serve as the assistant minister in Northampton, Massachusetts, alongside his 83-year-old maternal grandfather, the renowned Solomon Stoddard. The aging Stoddard was "the most influential clergyman in the region,"[30] but many felt that he needed assistance. Jonathan was ordained as his associate on Feb. 15, 1727, with the understanding that Stoddard would train young Edwards to succeed him. When Stoddard died two years later, Edwards was suddenly thrust into one of the most visible pulpits in New England at the age of twenty-six. He would pastor this church for the next twenty-two years, through both momentous and miserable times.

In the pulpit, Sunday by Sunday, Edwards soon distinguished himself as a preacher. His sermons were marked by "riveting expository skill . . . wide thematic range, a wealth of evangelical thought, a pervasive awareness of eternal issues, and a compelling logical flow to make them arresting, searching, devastating, and Christ-centeredly doxological to the last degree."[31] His preaching style was "commanding and by all accounts was almost hypnotic in its power to fix his hearers' minds on divine things."[32] During this time, Edwards also emerged as "a determined opponent of Arminianism."[33] Roger Olson remarks that "No theologian in the history of Christianity held a higher or stronger view of God's majesty, sovereignty, glory and power than Jonathan Edwards."[34] He "ardently defended the Puritan Calvinistic doctrines, . . . [declaring that] God is the all-determining reality in the most unconditional sense possible and always acts of His own glory and honor."[35]

One prime example of Edwards' staunch defense of Calvinistic doctrine was his address to the Puritan ministers of Boston in July 1731. The young preacher chose for his text 1 Corinthians 1:29–31, an unmistakable assertion of the absolute sovereignty of God in salvation. The message, titled "God Glorified in Man's Dependence," was designed to counter the growing influence of the man-centered Arminianism in his day. The Harvard alumni who gathered were impressed with the force of his argument, and the sermon soon became the first of Edwards' works to be published. Although Edwards had fought earlier against the biblical doctrine of divine sovereignty—a truth he once called a "horrible doctrine"[36]—through personal study, he had become convinced that God irresistibly orders the salvation of His chosen people, and he soon arose to be a guardian of this sacred truth.

In December 1734, a sovereign movement of God's Spirit came to New England. It began when Edwards preached a series of sermons on justification by faith, which was "directed against the tendency toward Arminianism . . . then developing in New England."[37] Through the winter months, nearly all the people of Northampton were seized by a deep concern for their souls, and more than three hundred professed faith in Christ. Edwards wrote: "The town seemed to be full of the presence of God; it never was so full of love, nor so full of joy. . . . There were remarkable tokens of God's presence in almost every house . . . everyone [was] earnestly intent on the public worship."[38]

After this intense revival (1734–1736), Edwards recorded its extraordinary effects in an eight-page letter to Benjamin Colman, a Boston minister. Edwards later expanded the content and Colman subsequently published it as *A Faithful Narrative of the Surprising Work of God in the Conversion of Many Hundred Souls in Northampton* (1736). This account soon reached London, where Isaac Watts, the gifted hymn writer, and John Guyse, a London minister, published it in England. Immediately, Edwards' influence was expanded overseas.

Summarizing the effects of the revival, Edwards wrote:

Our public assemblies were then beautiful, the congregation was then alive in God's service, everyone earnestly intent on the public worship, every hearer eager to drink in the words of the minister as they came from his mouth; the assembly in general were, from time to time in tears while the Word was preached; some weeping with sorrow and distress, others with joy and love, others with pity and concern for the souls of their neighbors.[39]

## THE AWAKENING REIGNITES (1740–1749)

A fuller measure of God's power came to the Colonies in 1740–1742. This movement, known as the Great Awakening, was linked with the itinerant preaching trips of the English evangelist George Whitefield, who traveled through the Colonies, calling people to repentance and faith. Edwards invited Whitefield to Northampton to preach, and he sat on the front pew and wept under the power of the great evangelist's pulpit ministry. Throughout New England, it is estimated that "out of a population of 300,000, between 25,000 and 50,000 new members were added to the churches"[40] during the revival.

In Edwards, the awakening had "a vigorous defender."[41] In fact, the awakening reached its height on July 8, 1741, when Edwards preached his most famous sermon. Titled "Sinners in the Hands of an Angry God," the sermon was based on Deuteronomy 32:35b: "their foot shall slide in due time" (KJV). Edwards had preached the sermon a month earlier in his own church with little visible effect. But when he delivered it at Enfield, a powerful revival occurred. Sinners were convicted and souls were shaken. Edwards was forced to motion for silence as people clung to the pews for fear of dropping into hell. Marsden comments: "What is extraordinary in this sermon is . . . the sustained imagery Edwards employs to pierce the hearts of the hearers. . . . He focuses everything on the central theme of what it means for guilty sinners to be held in the hands of God . . . they were left with no escape."[42]

But with the Great Awakening came much emotional excess. A controversy arose within the churches regarding the true nature of this movement. Many ministers opposed the revival; they were known as Old Lights, while the pastors who supported it were called New Lights. Yale College was torn down the middle. A turbulent meeting of the trustees was held Sept. 10, 1741. Edwards, providentially, was to deliver the commencement address the next day, and he gave his full support to the revival. In an exposition of 1 John 4:1–6, Edwards identified five marks by which an authentic work of the Spirit is to be recognized. Such a true work, he said, "(1) raises [people's] esteem of Jesus as Son of God and Savior of the world, (2) leads them to turn from their corruptions and lusts to the righteousness of God, (3) increases their regard for Holy Scripture, (4) establishes their minds in the objective truths of revealed religion, and (5) evokes genuine love for God and man."[43] Each of these, he believed, was present in the awakening. The message was published a month later under the title *The Distinguishing Marks of a Work of the Spirit of God* (1741) and was given a wide circulation.

Edwards again wrote on the subject of revival in a major work titled *Treatise Concerning Religious Affections* (1746). In this work, which became "the most important and accurate analysis of religious experience ever written . . . [Edwards] endeavored to identify what constitutes true and authentic spirituality."[44] He wrestled with the difference between true and false Christian experience, comparing what might not *necessarily* indicate saving faith with the true marks of conversion. This book is regarded by many historians as "the leading classic in American history on spiritual life."[45]

In these years, Edwards influenced an army of young men for the ministry. He preached the ordination sermons for numerous young ministers. Others lived with him, such as Joseph Bellamy, Samuel Buell, and Samuel Hopkins, who "became influential figures in New England."[46] One young man who stayed in the Edwards home was a daring missionary to the Delaware Indians in New Jersey and Pennsylvania, David Brainerd. In fact, Brainerd died of tuberculosis under Edwards' roof on Oct. 9, 1747. Edwards' daughter, Jerusha, was Brainerd's nurse in the home and, tragically, she contracted tuberculosis and died months later. Afterward, Jonathan edited and published Brainerd's diary, a record of his "selfless devotion to missions to the Indians."[47] Further, he wrote a biography of this young man, titled *An Account of the Life of the Rev. David Brainerd* (1749), which "helped inspire the missionary movement of the next century."[48]

## THE PAINFUL SEPARATION (1750)

Despite Edwards' ministry successes at Northampton for more than two decades, his distinguished pastorate came to an abrupt and bitter end in "one of the great mysteries of church history."[49] Stoddard, his predecessor and grandfather, had allowed people to take Communion based on a simple profession of Christ. Edwards became convinced "they must profess Christianity [and bring forth the fruits of conversion in their lives] before they could take Communion."[50] When Edwards tried to enforce this stronger standard, a firestorm developed in the church against him.

In a letter to his Scottish friend John Erskine in 1749, the year before his dismissal, Edwards reveals this mounting tension:

> A very great difficulty has arisen between me and my people, relating to qualifications for communion at the Lord's table. My honored grandfather Stoddard, my predecessor in the ministry over this church, strenuously maintained the Lord's Supper to be a converting ordinance, and urged all to come who were not of scandalous life, though they knew themselves to be unconverted. I formerly conformed to this practice, but I have had difficulties with respect to it, which have been long increasing; till I dared no longer in the former way: which has occasioned great uneasiness among my people, and has filled all the country with noise; which has obliged me to write something on the subject, which is now in the press. I know not but this affair will issue in a separation between me and my people. I desire your prayers that God would guide me in every step in this affair.[51]

The requirement of evidence of personal faith in Christ proved to be too much for the older members of Edwards' congregation. Several prominent families marshaled the majority and succeeded in having Edwards dismissed on June 22, 1750—truly one of the great tragedies of church history. Only 10 percent voted to keep Edwards as their pastor.[52]

The next Sunday, Edwards preached his farewell sermon from 2 Corinthians 1:14, speaking of that day when they would gather together before God as pastor and congregation and give an account to Him. Then, in a remarkable display of humility, Edwards remained at Northampton for a year, occasionally filling the pulpit until his successor could be found. Numerous ministry offers came to him, including invitations to pastor in prestigious places such as Boston and Scotland. A group of loyal supporters in Northampton even wished to start a new church there. But Edwards declined each of these offers. Once his replacement was found, he accepted a call to be the pastor and missionary to Native Americans at the frontier settlement of Stockbridge, Massachusetts.

## PIONEER MISSIONARY (1751–1757)

In the winter of 1751, Edwards moved to begin his new work with the Mohican and Mohawk Indians in the isolation of Stockbridge, some forty miles away. There Edwards faithfully pastored and preached the gospel to approximately 250 Indians and a dozen English families. In an irony of history, this towering intellectual genius communicated the gospel in a humble setting on the equivalent of a fifth-grade level.

Out of the public eye, Edwards experienced both highs and lows. Positively, God granted Edwards many converts and changed lives, but negatively, there was again conflict and controversy. The Williams family, which had caused him much trouble in Northampton, continued the fight in Stockbridge. Ephraim Williams, a thorn in Edwards' flesh, tried to smear Edwards' name, accusing him of embezzlement from the school established to teach the Indians. Although Edwards was cleared of wrongdoing, the Mohawks left the school, weary of the attacks against their leader. As a result, the school was forced to close and the mission was later ended.

But in these years, Edwards was given time to put his thoughts on paper. Spending thirteen hours a day in study, he wrote his three weightiest works: *Freedom of the Will* (1754), *The End for Which God Created the World* (1755; published with *True Virtue* under the title *The Two Treatises*), and *Original Sin* (1758). *Freedom of the Will*, his greatest literary achievement, was a monumental treatment of the inability of the fallen will to believe on Christ. In it, "Edwards argues that only the regenerate person can truly choose the transcendent God; that choice can be made only through a disposition that God infuses in regeneration."[53] The one who wills to believe in Christ, Edwards taught, is the one in whom the Holy Spirit has already performed His sovereign, monergistic work in the new birth.

## THE PRINCETON PRESIDENCY (1758)

Aaron Burr Sr.—Edwards' son-in-law, husband of his daughter Esther—was president of Princeton College, then known as the College of New Jersey. When Burr died in office on Sept. 24, 1757, the trustees turned to Edwards. Initially, Edwards declined their offer, insisting that he was unworthy for such a high position. But the trustees persisted, and despite some reluctance, Edwards accepted the presidency. He arrived in Princeton in January 1758, with Sarah remaining behind until the harsh winter had passed. On Feb. 16, 1758, Edwards was inaugurated the third president of Princeton, the school that would emerge as the greatest influence for orthodox theology in America in the nineteenth century.

Edwards then prepared to write what he believed would become his *magnum opus*, a theological work tracing the history of redemption through the Scriptures. But God had other plans. Within his first month as president, there was a smallpox outbreak, and Edwards chose to be inoculated to show others they need not fear this medical advance. In a strange providence, Edwards contracted a secondary infection and died March 22, but five weeks into his presidency. With only his daughters Esther and Lucy at his side, he whispered his last words:

It seems to me to be the will of God, that I must shortly leave you; therefore give my kindest love to my dear wife, and tell her, that the uncommon union, which has so long subsisted between us, has been of such a nature, as I trust is spiritual, and therefore will continue forever; and I hope she will be supported under so great a trial, and submit cheerfully to the will of God.[54]

Upon receiving the tragic news of Jonathan's death, Sarah wrote to Esther, who had lost both her husband and her father, in order to console her:

My very dear child, What shall I say? A holy and good God has covered us with a dark cloud. O that we may kiss the rod, and lay our hands upon our mouths! The Lord has done it. He has made me adore His goodness, that we had him so long. But my God lives; and He has my heart. O what a legacy my husband, and your father, has left us! We are all given to God; and there I am, and love to be.[55]

Esther herself died a few days later, on April 7, from a similar reaction to the smallpox vaccine. Sarah did not arrive in Princeton until that summer. When she did, she stood over the fresh graves of her son-in-law, her husband, and her daughter. Then she herself contracted dysentery and died Oct. 2, 1758. Sarah was buried next to her husband in the Princeton Cemetery.

## EDWARDS WAS RESOLVED

The legacy of Jonathan Edwards endures strong to this day. Historian Mark Noll concludes that Edwards produced "one of the most thorough and compelling bodies of theological writing in the history of America."[56] Through this corpus of work, this Colonial Puritan pastor speaks even louder to this generation than he did to his own time. His life exudes a moral excellence that is immediately apparent to all who study his remarkable history. To this day, Edwards remains "one of the great fathers of evangelical Christianity in America."[57]

Let us, then, return to our primary question: Why Edwards? What put him on a path to such greatness? The answer lies in this fact: Edwards possessed a rare combination of Reformed theology, extraordinary giftedness, and fervent piety. However, it was this latter virtue—his true spirituality, marked by a fixed resolve—that positioned him to be used so mightily by God. Few have equaled his relentless pursuit of personal holiness. Edwards' godliness fitted him to be the mighty instrument in the hand of God that he was.

It was in his late teens, while serving as an interim pastor in New York City, that Edwards recorded his "Resolutions," which would set the course for the rest of his life. Remarkably, Edwards strove to follow these seventy purpose statements until his last breath. In this sense, it is no secret why God used him as He did. Edwards was singularly focused on living the Christian life for God's glory. He was fully committed to honoring the Lord in *every* area of his life, and to doing so with an unwavering resolve.

What resolutions did Edwards record? What were his life priorities? What direction did they take him? I invite you to turn the page and discover the path that Edwards pursued in his quest for godliness.

## Notes

1. D. Martyn Lloyd-Jones, *The Puritans: Their Origins and Successors* (Edinburgh: Banner of Truth Trust, 1987, 1996), 355.
2. John Gerstner, *Jonathan Edwards: A Mini-Theology* (Morgan, Pa.: Soli Deo Gloria, 1987, 1996), 13.
3. Joel R. Beeke and Randall J. Pederson, *Meet the Puritans* (Grand Rapids: Reformation Heritage Books, 2006), 204.
4. Gerstner, *Jonathan Edwards: A Mini-Theology*, 13.
5. George Marsden, *Jonathan Edwards: A Life* (New Haven, Conn./London: Yale University Press, 2003), 1.
6. Benjamin B. Warfield, *The Works of Benjamin B. Warfield* (Grand Rapids: Baker, 1991), 9:515.
7. B. K. Kuiper, *The Church in History* (Grand Rapids: Eerdmans, 1951), 419.
8. Mark Noll, "Jonathan Edwards," *Evangelical Dictionary of Theology*, ed. Walter A. Elwell (Grand Rapids: Baker, 1984), 366.
9. Stephen J. Nichols, "Jonathan Edwards: His Life and Legacy," in *A God-Entranced Vision of All Things: The Legacy of Jonathan Edwards*, eds. John Piper and Justin Taylor (Wheaton, Ill.: Crossway, 2004), 43.
10. Noll, "Jonathan Edwards," *Evangelical Dictionary of Theology*, 366.
11. Curt Daniel, *The History and Theology of Calvinism* (Dallas, Texas: Scholarly Reprints, 1993), 99.
12. Marsden, *Jonathan Edwards: A Life*, 1.
13. R. C. Sproul, book jacket, *The Freedom of the Will* (Morgan, Pa.: Soli Deo Gloria, 1996).
14. Paul Ramsey, "Editor's Introduction," *Jonathan Edwards: Freedom of the Will*, ed. Paul Ramsey (New Haven, Conn./London: Yale University Press, 1957, 1985), 2.

15. For further information, see Elisabeth D. Dodds, *Marriage to a Difficult Man: The Uncommon Union of Jonathan and Sarah Edwards* (Philadelphia: Westminster Press, 1976), 202–214.

16. S. M. Houghton, *Sketches from Church History* (Edinburgh: Banner of Truth Trust, 1980, 2001), 182.

17. Meic Pearse, *The Age of Reason: From the Wars of Religion to the French Revolution* (Grand Rapids: Baker, 2006), 342.

18. Harry S. Stout, as quoted in Stephen J. Nichols, *Jonathan Edwards: A Guided Tour of His Life and Thought* (Phillipsburg, N.J.: P&R, 2001), 17.

19. Lloyd-Jones, *The Puritans: Their Origins and Successors*, 356.

20. Ibid.

21. Ibid.

22. David Vaughn, *A Divine Light: The Spiritual Leadership of Jonathan Edwards* (Nashville: Cumberland House, 2007), 144.

23. Nichols, *Jonathan Edwards: A Guided Tour of His Life and Thought*, 30.

24. George S. Claghorn, "Introduction," *The Works of Jonathan Edwards, Vol. 16, Letters and Personal Writings*, ed. George S. Claghorn (New Haven, Conn.: Yale University Press, 1998), 744.

25. Ibid.

26. Jonathan Edwards, "Personal Narrative," as quoted in Iain Murray, *Jonathan Edwards: A New Biography* (Edinburgh: Banner of Truth Trust, 1987), 35–36.

27. Ibid.

28. Jonathan Edwards, quoted in Dale and Sandy Larsen, *Jonathan Edwards: Renewed Heart* (Downers Grove, Ill.: InterVarsity, 2002), 8.

29. Stephen J. Nichols, *Jonathan Edwards' Resolutions and Advice to Young Converts* (Phillipsburg, N.J.: P&R, 2001), 5.

30. George Marsden, "Biography," *The Cambridge Companion to Jonathan Edwards*, ed. Stephen J. Stein (Cambridge/New York: Cambridge University Press, 2007), 25.

31. J. I. Packer, "The Glory of God in the Reviving of Religion," in *A God-Entranced Vision of All Things: The Legacy of Jonathan Edwards*, 84.

32. Ibid.

33. Tony Lane, *A Concise History of Christian Thought* (Grand Rapids: Baker, 2006), 188.

34. Roger E. Olson, *The Story of Christian Theology* (Downers Grove, Ill.: InterVarsity, 1999), 506.

35. Ibid.

36. Edwards, "Personal Narrative," as quoted in Marsden, *Jonathan Edwards: A Life*, 40.

37. Kuiper, *The Church in History*, 420.

38. Quoted in Stephen J. Nichols, "A Mind on Fire," *Christian History*, Issue 77, 12.

39. Jonathan Edwards, *A Faithful Narrative of the Surprising Work of God*, in *The Works of Jonathan Edwards, Vol. 4: The Great Awakening*, ed. C. C. Goen (New Haven, Conn.: Yale University Press, 1972), 151.

40. Kuiper, *The Church in History*, 420.

41. Bruce L. Shelley, "The Great Awakening," *The New International Dictionary of the Christian Church*, gen. ed. J. D. Douglas (Grand Rapids: Zondervan, 1974, 1978), 429.

42. Marsden, *Jonathan Edwards: A Life*, 222.

43. Edwards, *The Distinguishing Marks of a Work of the Spirit of God*, in *Works* (Yale), *Vol. 4*, 54.

44. Samuel Storms, *Signs of the Spirit: An Interpretation of Jonathan Edwards' Religious Affections* (Wheaton, Ill.: Crossway 2007), 21.

45. Beeke and Pederson, *Meet the Puritans*, 226.

46. Nichols, *Jonathan Edwards: A Guided Tour of His Life and Thought*, 580.

47. Marsden, "Biography," *The Cambridge Companion to Jonathan Edwards*, 33.

48. Ibid.

49. Nichols, *Jonathan Edwards: A Guided Tour of His Life and Thought*, 60.

50. Mark Dever, "How Jonathan Edwards Got Fired, and Why It's Important for Us Today," in *A God-Entranced Vision of All Things: The Legacy of Jonathan Edwards*, 133.

51. As quoted by Nichols in *Jonathan Edwards: A Guided Tour of His Life and Thought*, 61.

52. Dever, "How Jonathan Edwards Got Fired, and Why It's Important for Us Today," in *A God-Entranced Vision of All Things: The Legacy of Jonathan Edwards*, 129.

53. Beeke and Pederson, *Meet the Puritans*, 203.

54. Edwards, as quoted by Dodds in *Marriage to a Difficult Man*, 160.

55. Sereno E. Dwight, "Memoir," in Jonathan Edwards, *The Works of Jonathan Edwards, Vol. 1* (Edinburgh: Banner of Truth Trust, 1974), 178.

56. Noll, "Jonathan Edwards," *Evangelical Dictionary of Theology*, 366.

57. John Piper, *God's Passion for His Glory: Living the Vision of Jonathan Edwards* (Wheaton, Ill: Crossway, 1998), 23.

# CHAPTER TWO

# A Spiritual Compass for the Soul

*The intensity of [Edwards'] inner life in these early years was extraordinary. His famous "Resolutions" capture some of the remarkable passion of this season of his life. There was a single-mindedness that governed his life and enabled him to accomplish amazing things.*[1]

—JOHN PIPER

God has given to His church a small number of men who have lived with such spiritual profundity that they have, as Sereno E. Dwight writes, "stamped their own image on the minds of succeeding generations."[2] These luminous figures have been sovereignly placed by God on the stage of human history in their appointed hours to cast long shadows of influence. Typically, they have risen far above one local congregation, leading ministries that have extended far beyond a single place. They have belonged not merely to their own hours, but to all ages. Such a man was Jonathan Edwards.

Possessing immense intellectual powers, Edwards "saw truth almost intuitively."[3] Few have been more proficient in handling Scripture, and only a handful in history have been as skilled in tracing doctrinal and philosophical themes. However, Edwards stands out not merely for his genius but for his godliness. Steeped in Puritan piety and stamped with singular devotion to God, he purposed to love and follow Jesus Christ to the utmost of his ability. Perhaps none so intellectually endowed has been as firmly determined in the pursuit of holiness as Edwards.

When Edwards was eighteen years old, having been recently converted, he determined to pursue and promote the glory of God with his entire being. Over the course of approximately one year, from around late summer 1722 to Aug. 17, 1723, he crafted his "Resolutions," a personal mission statement that would guide and discipline him in this pursuit of godliness. The "Resolutions" reveal the steely determination with which he sought to direct his steps. For Edwards, George Claghorn writes, the "Resolutions" were "neither pious hopes, romantic dreams, nor legalistic rules."[4] Instead, they were intensely positive and practical, comprising "instructions for life, maxims to be followed in all respects."[5] The "Resolutions" reveal Edwards' "strong sense of duty and discipline, in private and public matters, in intellect and spirituality."[6] Collectively, they form an emphatic statement, Stephen Nichols notes, of how he sought to "chart out his life—his relationships, his conversations, his desires, his activities."[7]

In this chapter, we will survey the distinctive features of the "Resolutions" in order to gain a general orientation to the seventy pledges as a whole.

## HISTORICAL SETTING

Any introduction to the "Resolutions" should begin by addressing the historical setting in which they were written. When did Edwards set down these goals? What were the circumstances of his life at the time? What were the factors that led to their writing? Did Edwards write them all at once or over a period of time? Knowing the historical context in which the "Resolutions" were composed will aid our understanding and appreciation of them.

In 1722, when Edwards was eighteen, he had completed two years of class work toward his master's degree at Yale College. All that remained before his graduation was the writing of his thesis on the doctrine of imputation, a paper titled "A Sinner is Not Justified in the Sight of God Except Through the Righteousness of Christ Obtained by Faith."[8] At this time, he traveled to New York City to serve as the interim pastor of First Presbyterian Church, a small Scottish Presbyterian congregation located near what is today Wall Street. His nine-month tenure there, from early August 1722 to the end of April 1723, proved to be critically important to Edwards' newly begun Christian walk.

A Christian for only a year, having been converted in the spring of 1721, Edwards was conscious that his faith in Christ needed direction. This was the first time he had lived outside the familiar confines of the Connecticut River Valley. In this strange place, without the structure of home or school, he sensed that he needed spiritual discipline to match the new freedom that he was afforded. Further, as a young minister, Edwards felt the heavy weight of pastoral responsibility upon his inexperienced shoulders. How he would minister was of great concern to him. Moreover, Edwards was wrestling with his vocational calling: Would God have him teach in the world of academics or serve the local church as a pastor?

All this prompted Edwards to begin writing his "Resolutions" to help direct his heart and life in godliness. The process required approximately one year. The first dated resolution was number 35, dated Dec. 18, 1722, which is around the time when his diary commences.[9] Thus, the first thirty-four resolutions were written before this date. Dwight explains: "The first twenty-one were written at once, with the same pen; as were the next ten, at a subsequent sitting. The rest were written occasionally. They were all on two detached pieces of paper."[10] It is thought that the first twenty-one resolutions were written earlier in 1722, while Edwards was still at Yale, or, more probably, that fall.[11] Other resolutions followed as Edwards sensed the need to govern his spirituality in new areas. He penned the last resolution on Aug. 17, 1723, two months before his twentieth birthday.

Consequently, the majority of Edwards' resolutions, if not all, were composed during his New York interim pastorate and then during a brief stay at home prior to receiving his master's degree in September 1723. As can be seen, the "Resolutions" were written at a "transitional time"[12] in Edwards' young adult life, when "he was moving from his foundational and formative years as a student to the period in which he began his profession as a churchman and theologian."[13]

## CULTURAL PRECEDENCE

Edwards' attempt to write a collection of resolutions was not without cultural precedence. Iain Murray notes, "New though this was to Edwards, it was not new in the least to the Christian tradition of New England."[14] Others in the Puritan Colonies had adopted this practice, especially the learned. Kenneth Minkema writes, "The discipline of making lists of resolutions was fairly common in Edwards' time"[15] because the Puritan age was a time of pursuing self-mastery in one's life. Claghorn observes, "Drawing up resolutions was a standard practice for educated people in the eighteenth century."[16]

One example was Benjamin Franklin (1706–1790), a founding father of the United States and a leading author, printer, politician, statesman, diplomat, scientist, and inventor.

As a young man, Franklin drew up a list of thirteen moral virtues that he purposed to pursue in daily living. Although Franklin was never converted to Christ, he nevertheless sought to be an outwardly moral person.

It should be noted that "scholars have long compared Edwards' and Benjamin Franklin's resolutions,"[17] even though Franklin's list was significantly shorter than Edwards' and certainly not as heart searching.[18] Both men agreed on the value of drafting resolutions, evaluating themselves accordingly, and following them throughout life. Franklin's fourth virtue even uses vocabulary very similar to what Edwards employs in his "Resolutions." Franklin wrote: "4. Resolution. Resolve to perform what you ought; perform without fail what you resolve."[19] But Franklin represented the Age of Reason, with its emphasis on this world and good citizenship. His virtues were "brief, epigrammatic, and eclectic,"[20] with Jesus and Socrates meriting equal imitation. By contrast, Edwards was the exemplar of Puritanism, depicting himself as weak and sinful, helpless without divine grace. The ultimate intention of Edwards' "Resolutions" was to "produce a soul fit for eternity with God . . . [as he] adjured himself to study the Scriptures, and pray steadfastly; Jesus was to be trusted as Lord; God was present, personal, and primary."[21]

Moreover, George Washington (1732–1799), the first president of the United States, copied 110 "Rules of Civility" into his school notebook in hopes of living a disciplined life. But again, there was a great difference between Washington's list and Edwards'. Washington was "cultivating personal morality . . . [with the goal of] becoming socially acceptable."[22] By contrast, Edwards' "Resolutions" partook of "Puritan self-discipline and self-abasement,"[23] and were designed to help him become not merely good but godly. The Puritan age was one of strict discipline, and Edwards embraced it.

## SPIRITUAL PURPOSE

Edwards had two chief goals in mind as he penned his guidelines for pursuing godliness. Both of these aims were firmly rooted in the overarching spiritual purpose of seeking God's glory.

First, the "Resolutions" represented Edwards' "firm determination"[24] to keep spiritual priorities continually before him. Because Edwards' spiritual eye was riveted on eternity, Minkema notes, the seventy resolutions are "all composed with one goal—heaven."[25] George Marsden writes, "Many of the resolutions are directed toward trying never to lose focus on spiritual things."[26] Edwards desired to bring *all* areas of his life under the Lordship of Jesus Christ through rigorous self-mastery. No part of life could be ignored or left unchallenged. The "Resolutions" are "straightforward statements of purpose"[27] in which "he offers himself his own advice."[28] In other words, Edwards' "Resolutions" constituted personal vows to himself, pledges to pursue holiness. In them, Edwards stated how he desired to walk daily before the Lord. Thus, they helped him set his course toward unwavering devotion to God.

To be sure, the "Resolutions" never lose sight of their practicality for daily living. Murray asserts, "Nothing shows more clearly the new prevailing bent of Edwards' mind and heart than his seventy 'Resolutions.'"[29] In short, the "Resolutions," Philip F. Gura explains, were "to guide him in living the Christian life."[30]

Second, the "Resolutions" were to serve as "guidelines for self-examination"[31] by which Edwards could keep his finger on the pulse of his spiritual life. The Puritans sought to "submit themselves to divine searching and to monitor their motives and actions."[32] These devout believers aimed to "practice introspection as a duty of great consequence."[33] Standing firmly in this tradition, Edwards believed that only by regularly examining his life could he adequately pursue the glory of God.

Thus, Edwards expected that his "Resolutions" would provide the spiritual criteria by which he would carefully probe his inner life. He intended them to be a window into his soul, a useful tool to help him excavate the depths of his heart, leaving no stone unturned. As Nichols explains, the "Resolutions" would be "a system of checks and balances that would be used to chart out his life."[34] They would serve as a personal audit by which he could evaluate the direction, vitality, and progress of his Christian walk.

## THEOLOGICAL ROOTS

All Christian writing is influenced, to one extent or another, by the theological foundations upon which the author stands. Edwards' writings, including his "Resolutions," rested squarely upon "Reformed theology in its English Puritan form."[35] This theological system, which emphasized God's glory and absolute sovereignty, "provided a structural framework for Edwards' thought."[36] In short, Edwards was a "convinced Calvinist";[37] he had drunk deeply from the wells of Scripture and had tasted the supreme authority of God to his soul's satisfaction. It is safe to say that few in the history of Christianity have held a higher view of God's majesty, sovereignty, glory, and power than Edwards. He unequivocally possessed a "God-entranced worldview of all things,"[38] one that, as J. I. Packer puts it, was "God-centered, God-focused, God-intoxicated, and God-entranced."[39]

Two classic works—the Westminster Shorter Catechism (1648) and John Calvin's *Institutes of the Christian Religion* (1559)—especially shaped Edwards' thinking during his formative years. As a result, Edwards' "Resolutions" became a practical expression of his daily effort to live out Reformed theology on a personal, experiential level.

Edwards' father, Timothy, taught him the Shorter Catechism while he was in grammar school. In college at Yale, Edwards received further exposure to this teaching standard and embraced its Reformed perspective on predestination, providence, and other doctrines. Thus, when Edwards took his pen in hand to write his "Resolutions," the rich theology of the Shorter Catechism came flowing out, emphasizing God's sovereignty, providence, and decrees, as well as such doctrines as unconditional election, total depravity, irresistible grace, and God's eternal preservation of His saints.

The theological similarities between Edwards' "Resolutions" and the Shorter Catechism are noticeable. William S. Morris, an Edwardian scholar, observes that the first resolution is almost "a free translation into more philosophic language of the First and Forty-second Questions and Answers in the Westminster Catechism."[40] The first question of the Shorter Catechism asks, "What is the chief end of man?"[41] The answer is, "Man's chief end is to glorify God, and to enjoy him for ever."[42] It is not by accident that Edwards' "Resolutions" begin at this point—the glory of God. Three of the first four resolutions, in fact, are strong, declarative statements of Edwards' desire to live for the glory of God.

Likewise, a reading of Edwards' "Resolutions" quickly reveals the influence of Calvin's *Institutes* upon his thinking. The *Institutes* was Calvin's *magnum opus*, a monumental work that he expanded from a relatively small edition of six chapters in its first printing (1536) to a large tome of seventy-nine chapters (1559). The central theme of the *Institutes* is the glory of God. The Genevan Reformer begins with a study of the transcendent greatness of God, arguing that only by knowing

God can man gain true knowledge of himself. Morris writes that the reader of the "Resolutions" is struck "by the fact that it harmonizes so well with what Calvin had said of the life of the Christian in the *Institutes*."[43] Morris points out that there is a noticeable overlap of Book III, sections 6 through 10, of the *Institutes* with several of Edwards' resolutions. Glorifying God was the highest aim of the Reformation, and it became the apex of Edwards' "Resolutions," as well.

Furthermore, Morris notes that the influence of Calvin and his *Institutes* can be seen specifically in those areas of the "Resolutions" dealing with "self-humiliation (no. 8), conquest of pride and vanity (no. 12), active benevolence to neighbors (no. 13), temperance in matters of food and drink (nos. 20 and 40), constant self-examination (*passion*), the control and directions of the affections (nos. 45, 47, 52, 59, 60, 61, 64, 68), and the use of afflictions (no. 67)."[44]

## MAJOR CATEGORIES

In terms of overall structure, the "Resolutions," for the most part, have no noticeable progression of thought from one resolution to the next. However, particular resolutions may be grouped according to theological themes or practical topics. Minkema observes one such possible grouping:

> The "Resolutions" . . . generally fell into several
> categories. Some dealt with specific habits, such as

"improving" time (no. 5), maximizing study (no. 11), controlling diet (nos. 20, 40), reading the Scriptures (no. 28), and combating "listlessness" (no. 61). Others, going deeper into the self, pertained to examining motives, tracing back an action to "the original intention, designs and ends of it" (nos. 23, 24). These included revenge (no. 14), speaking ill of others (nos. 16, 31, 36), profaning the Sabbath (no. 38), and dishonoring parents (no. 46).[45]

For this study, Edwards' seventy resolutions will be organized around six main headings, which will be considered in chapters 4 through 9, respectively. They are as follows:

• *Pursuing the Glory of God.* As noted above, this was Edwards' chief priority. Minkema writes, "Glorifying God in every thought, word, and deed"[46] was paramount for Edwards. So important was this goal for him that he purposed to "do whatsoever I think to be most to God's glory" (no. 1) and "to be continually endeavoring to find out some new invention and contrivance to promote [the glory of God]" (no. 2). Edwards vowed "never to do any manner of thing . . . but what tends to the glory of God" (no. 4). Later, he added a pledge "never willfully to omit anything, except the omission be for the glory of God" (no. 27).

• *Forsaking Sin.* Edwards understood that if he was to glorify God, he must forsake sin. He pledged that if he should ever "fall and grow dull, so as to neglect to keep any part of these Resolutions," he would repent (no. 3). He vowed to trace every iniquity "back . . . to the original cause" in his heart (no. 24). Edwards purposed "never to speak" what is improper "on the Lord's day" (no. 38). In short, he was determined that his conscience should remain clean. With steadfast determination, he pledged "never to give over . . . [in] my fight with my corruptions" (no. 56), but "to confess frankly to myself . . . [and] to God" all sin within (no. 68).

Other resolutions concerned the restraint of his anger, apparently an area in which he felt a sharp need to gain mastery. Edwards purposed "never to suffer the least motions of anger to irrational beings" (no. 15). He pledged that he would "endeavor to my utmost to deny whatever is not most agreeable to a good . . . temper" (no. 47), and he determined, when suffering "provocations to ill-nature and anger, . . . [to strive to act] good-naturedly" (no. 59). Edwards was determined to resist sin in all its various forms in his life, especially anger.

• *Making Proper Use of God-Allotted Time.* It is clear that use of time was vitally important to Edwards because he positioned resolutions on this matter early in his list. As Claghorn observes, "His aim was to rise early, work late, and fill every moment with constructive activity."[47] Edwards pledged "never to lose one moment of time" (no. 5), purposing to "not give way to . . . listlessness, . . . [which] relaxes my mind from being fully and fixedly set on religion" (no. 61).

Edwards was motivated to use his time well because he had a strong realization that he stood each moment on the brink of eternity. He deliberately chose to think about "the common circumstances which attend death" (no. 9). He determined to live as he would in the hour "before I should hear the last trump" (no. 19) and as he would judge proper "when I come into the future world" (no. 50). He aimed to live without regrets, "supposing I live to old age" (no. 52). To promote this perspective, he resolved to imagine how he would live had he already seen "the happiness of heaven, and hell torments" (no. 55).

• *Living with All His Being for the Lord.* Edwards resolved "to live with all my might, while I do live" (no. 6). He vowed to "cast away" all that might steal his assurance (no. 26). Edwards also pledged himself to "study the Scriptures . . . steadily, constantly and frequently" (no. 28). And he committed himself to "strive to my utmost . . . to be brought . . . to a higher exercise of grace" (no. 30).

Edwards vowed he would regularly "renew the dedication of myself to God" (no. 42), that he would act as if he were "entirely and altogether God's" (no. 43), and that "no other end but religion . . . [should] influence" him (no. 44). Further, Edwards determined that he would permit into his life only such "pleasure or grief, joy or sorrow" as would help his practice of "religion" (no. 45). Despite challenges, he resolved to "cast . . . my soul on the Lord Jesus Christ . . . [and] trust and confide in him" (no. 53). Edwards wrote that if there was "one individual in the world, at any one time, who was properly a complete Christian," he would strive "to be that one, who should live in my time" (no. 63). With abandonment, he stated that he would "declare my ways to God, and lay open my soul to him" (no. 65). In summary, Edwards set himself to live a God-centered life focused on the Lord Jesus Christ.

Such abandonment to live to the fullest would necessitate even moderation in his diet. Edwards believed that God was to be glorified in everything, even in consuming food and drink (1 Cor. 10:31). Thus, he resolved "to maintain the strictest temperance in eating and drinking" (no. 20), and he purposed to "inquire every night" whether he had acted "in the best way I possibly could, with respect to eating and drinking" (no. 40). Even this mundane area of life must be managed for the glory of God.

• *Pursuing Humility and Love.* Edwards knew that he could not glorify God with pride or hatred in his heart. Therefore, he resolved to act "as if nobody had been so vile as I, and as if I had committed the same sins . . . as others" (no. 8). Such a lifestyle, he recognized, would necessitate that he throw off "pride" and "vanity" (no. 12).

Further, Edwards purposed to demonstrate love toward others. Specifically, this included striving to live with "charity and liberality" (no. 13) and "never to do anything out of revenge" (no. 14), "never to speak evil of anyone" (no. 16), "never to say anything at all against anybody" improperly (no. 31), and to be always "making, maintaining and establishing peace" (no. 33). Further, Edwards pledged to exercise love toward his parents so as "never to allow the least measure of any fretting uneasiness at my father or mother" (no. 46).

• *Making Frequent Self-Examination.* Edwards pledged to "examine carefully, and constantly" what caused him "to doubt of the love of God" (no. 25). He vowed to "inquire every night . . . what sin I have committed" (no. 37) and "to ask myself at the end of every day, week, month and year . . . [how he could have] done better" (no. 41). He specifically set himself to "examine strictly every week" his temper (no. 47). He pledged to look, with "strictest scrutiny," into the condition of his soul for true "interest in Christ" (no. 48). If he feared misfortune, he determined to "examine whether I have done my duty" (no. 57). When his feelings were "out of order" or he was uneasy, he determined that he would "subject myself to the strictest examination" (no. 60).

## COMPLEMENTARY WRITINGS

At the same time Edwards was writing his "Resolutions," he was recording his diary and "The Miscellanies." He later wrote his "Personal Narrative," in which he looked back upon this early time in his life. Any consideration of the "Resolutions" necessitates interacting with these three supporting sources.

Edwards' diary records intensely personal feelings about his efforts to follow his "Resolutions." It is "the most important biographical source dating from the New York period,"[48] giving an inside look into Edwards' life as he began to live out his purpose statements. The diary contains 148 entries in which he "bares his soul about his struggles"[49] to keep the

"Resolutions." "Like an X-ray of the soul,"[50] they are "a revelation of his feelings and efforts"[51] as he began his Christian life. Recorded in the diary is a full range of emotions, of "both triumph and defeat."[52] In some entries, he professes himself to be "exceedingly, dull, dry, and dead"[53] and "overwhelmed with melancholy."[54] In others, he shows himself to be exultant with awe, wonder, and thankfulness toward God.

Edwards began "The Miscellanies" in 1722, the year he started his "Resolutions." It would remain a work in progress for the rest of his life. This project included both "one-sentence thoughts" and "page-long reflections."[55] "The Miscellanies" consisted of "papers and folders to which he was to be constantly adding throughout his life"[56]—philosophical statements, exegetical notes, and records of spiritual experiences and even scientific explorations. But one subject in "The Miscellanies" outweighs all others, that which "never ceased to be first in his concerns"[57]—the pursuit of holiness. This same focus on sanctification occupied his mind in the composition of his "Resolutions."

In 1740, when Edwards was thirty-seven years old, he wrote his "Personal Narrative." Of all that Edwards wrote, "nothing provides the penetrating gaze into his own soul, together with his spiritual struggles and triumphs,"[58] as does the "Personal Narrative." It gives insight into his relationship with God, in response to a letter from his future son-in-law, Aaron Burr Sr., and serves as a short spiritual autobiography. Edwards' reflections in "Personal Narrative" on the earlier years of his life are vitally important in understanding the "Resolutions."

## THE PASSIONATE PURSUIT OF GODLINESS

As a young man, Jonathan Edwards purposed to order his spiritual life by vowing to live for the glory of God. Such resolve would require him to live with spiritual discipline and a dogged determination in every area of life. He knew that in this pursuit, sin must be forsaken and his tendency to anger resisted. Time must be measured, death must be appraised, and eternity weighed. Life must be lived wholeheartedly. Humility must be shown and love practiced. In all this, self must be regularly examined.

At the very beginning of his Christian journey, Edwards asked himself: How do I want to live? What is my purpose in life? What type of person do I want to be? His answers to these questions were framed in his "Resolutions."

No matter where we are in our individual Christian lives, none of us has arrived. There is much spiritual maturity yet to be realized. There is much more that God can do in and through us. Edwards' approach to the Christian life serves as a strong motivation for each of us to live for the glory of God. May you resolve to live your life not for self but for God.

### Notes

1. John Piper, *God's Passion For His Glory: Living the Vision of Jonathan Edwards* (Wheaton, Ill.: Crossway, 1998), 52.
2. Sereno E. Dwight, "Memoir," in Jonathan Edwards, *The Works of Jonathan Edwards, Vol. 1* (Edinburgh: Banner of Truth Trust, 1974), xi.

3. Ibid.

4. George S. Claghorn, "Introduction," Jonathan Edwards, *The Works of Jonathan Edwards, Vol. 16, Letters and Personal Writings,* ed. George S. Claghorn (New Haven, Conn.: Yale University Press, 1998), 741.

5. Ibid.

6. M. X. Lesser, *Reading Jonathan Edwards: An Annotated Bibliography in Three Parts, 1729–2005* (Grand Rapids/Cambridge: Eerdmans, 2008), 245.

7. Stephen J. Nichols, *Jonathan Edwards' Resolutions and Advice to Young Converts* (Phillipsburg, N.J.: P&R, 2001), 5.

8. Jonathan Edwards, *The Works of Jonathan Edwards, Vol. 14, Sermons and Discourses, 1723–1729,* ed. Kenneth P. Minkema (New Haven, Conn.: Yale University Press, 1997), 60–66.

9. Edwards, "Diary," *Works* (Yale), *Vol. 16,* 759.

10. Dwight, "Memoir," in *The Works of Jonathan Edwards, Vol.1,* xxiv.

11. Samuel Storms, *Signs of the Spirit: An Interpretation of Jonathan Edwards' Religious Affections* (Wheaton, Ill.: Crossway, 2007), 217.

12. Nichols, *Jonathan Edwards' Resolutions,* 11.

13. Ibid.

14. Iain Murray, *Jonathan Edwards: A New Biography* (Edinburgh: Banner of Truth Trust, 1987), 42.

15. Kenneth P. Minkema, "Personal Writings," in *The Cambridge Companion to Jonathan Edwards,* ed. Stephen J. Stein (Cambridge/New York: Cambridge University Press, 2007), 40.

16. Claghorn, "Introduction," *Works* (Yale), *Vol. 16,* 741.

17. Ibid., 742.

18. Franklin's virtues are listed in his autobiography. This work originally was published in Paris as *Memoires De La Vie Privee* one year after Franklin's death. It was then published two years later in English as *The Private Life of the Late Benjamin Franklin, LL.D.* (1793). Today it is known as *The Autobiography of Benjamin Franklin.*

19. Benjamin Franklin, *The Autobiography of Benjamin Franklin* (New York: Touchstone, 1962, 2004), 67.

20. Claghorn, "Introduction," *Works* (Yale), *Vol. 16,* 743.

21. Ibid., 742–743.

22. Minkema, "Personal Writings," *The Cambridge Companion to Jonathan Edwards,* 40.

23. Ibid.

24. Claghorn, "Introduction," *Works* (Yale), *Vol. 16,* 741.

25. Minkema, "Personal Writings," *The Cambridge Companion to Jonathan Edwards*, 40.

26. George Marsden, *Jonathan Edwards: A Life* (New Haven, Conn./London: Yale University Press, 2003), 50.

27. Claghorn, "Introduction," *Works* (Yale), *Vol. 16*, 743.

28. Nichols, *Jonathan Edwards' Resolutions*, 5.

29. Murray, *Jonathan Edwards: A New Biography*, 42.

30. Philip F. Gura, *Jonathan Edwards: America's Evangelical* (New York: Hill and Wang, 2005), 31.

31. Claghorn, "Introduction," *Works* (Yale), *Vol. 16*, 741.

32. Ibid.

33. Ibid.

34. Nichols, *Jonathan Edwards' Resolutions*, 5.

35. Thomas A. Schafer, "Editor's Introduction," *The Works of Jonathan Edwards, Vol. 13, The Miscellanies (Entry Nos. 1-z, aa-zz, 1-500)*, ed. Thomas A. Schafer (New Haven, Conn.: Yale University Press, 1996), 39.

36. Ibid.

37. Justo L. Gonzalez, *A History of Christian Thought: From the Protestant Reformation to the Twentieth Century* (Nashville: Abingdon Press, 1975), 288.

38. Mark Noll, "Jonathan Edwards, Moral Philosophy, and the Secularization of American Christian Thought," *Reformed Journal*, 33 (February 1983), 26.

39. J. I. Packer, "The Glory of God and the Reviving of Religion," *A God-Entranced Vision of All Things: The Legacy of Jonathan Edwards*, eds. John Piper and Justin Taylor (Wheaton, Ill.: Crossway, 2004), 86.

40. William S. Morris, *The Young Jonathan Edwards: A Reconstruction* (Eugene, Ore.: Wipf & Stock, 2005), 44.

41. "The Shorter Catechism," *The Westminster Confession of Faith* (Atlanta: Committee for Christian Education & Publications, 1990), 3.

42. Ibid.

43. Morris, *The Young Jonathan Edwards*, 44.

44. Ibid., 45.

45. Minkema, "Personal Writings," *The Cambridge Companion to Jonathan Edwards*, 40.

46. Ibid.

47. Claghorn, "Introduction," *Works* (Yale), *Vol. 16*, 744.

48. Murray, *Jonathan Edwards: A New Biography*, 44.

49. Claghorn, "Introduction," *Works* (Yale), *Vol. 16*, 743.

50. Stephen J. Nichols, *Jonathan Edwards: A Guided Tour of His Life and Thought* (Phillipsburg, N.J.: P&R, 2001), 39.
51. Claghorn, "Introduction," *Works* (Yale), *Vol. 16*, 743.
52. Nichols, *Jonathan Edwards: A Guided Tour of His Life and Thought*, 39.
53. Edwards, "Diary," *Works* (Yale), *Vol. 16*, 759.
54. Ibid., 765.
55. Nichols, *Jonathan Edwards: A Guided Tour of His Life and Thought*, 39.
56. Murray, *Jonathan Edwards: A New Biography*, 42.
57. Ibid., 50.
58. Storms, *Signs of the Spirit: An Interpretation of Jonathan Edwards' Religious Affections*, 155.

# CHAPTER THREE

# The Prerequisite of Faith

*The clue to Edwards then, his dominating and irradiating quality, the trait which gave unity to his career, is his spirituality.*[1]

—JOHN DEWITT

As Jonathan Edwards penned his "Resolutions," he was keenly aware that God alone is the Agent of sanctification. While he knew he was responsible to obey God's Word and pursue holiness, he understood that he could not do so by sheer will power. Edwards wrote his seventy vows "to keep his heart pure and dedicated to Christ,"[2] knowing that he could do it *only* by the grace of God through the enablement of the indwelling Holy Spirit.

Edwards acknowledged his dependence on God in a two-sentence introduction to the "Resolutions." This "preamble" reveals much about Edwards' theology, providing valuable insight into how he viewed God, himself, and the Christian life. While the seventy resolutions reveal *what* he purposed to do, the preamble indicates *how* he would do it. He recognized that he must depend on God to fulfill his spiritual duty, as spelled out in the "Resolutions."

Sereno E. Dwight, an early Edwards biographer, notes the critical importance of the preamble: "This he places at the head of all his other important rules that his whole dependence was on the grace of God."[3] Stephen Nichols agrees, writing, "Far from an advocate for self-help, Edwards realizes that anything he might do that pleases God or anything that amounts to something of significance is only the result of God working through him."[4] That is to say, Edwards agreed with the apostle Paul, who wrote, "By the grace of God I am what I am" (1 Cor. 15:10). Only by sanctifying grace, and not by his autonomous efforts, could Edwards "walk in a manner worthy of [his] calling" (Eph. 4:1).

The preamble is a brief but precise acknowledgement of Edwards' humble dependence upon God in the pursuit of godliness. It reads:

Being sensible that I am unable to do anything without God's help, I do humbly entreat him by his grace to enable me to keep these Resolutions, so far as they are agreeable to his will, for Christ's sake.

Remember to read over these Resolutions once a week.

In this chapter, we will examine these sentences phrase by phrase, and at times even word by word, to grasp the significance of Edwards' approach to growth in godliness in the Christian life. As we work our way through the preamble, we will consider five key observations that give insight into how Edwards hoped to keep his "Resolutions."

## PERSONAL INABILITY

At the beginning of the preamble, Edwards acknowledged that he was unable to accomplish any spiritual good on his own. He wrote, "Being sensible that I am unable to do anything without God's help. . . ." The word *sensible* indicates awareness. Edwards knew he lacked the ability to "do anything" pleasing to God or to produce his own spiritual growth.[5]

Thus, the preamble shows that Edwards knew he could not fulfill his "Resolutions" by simply resolving to do so. Composing these vows did not indicate that he presumed to possess the natural ability to keep them. Edwards "was too well acquainted with human weakness and frailty even where the intentions are most sincere, to enter on any resolutions rashly, or from a reliance on his own strength."[6]

In his diary, Edwards bared his soul regarding his helplessness to achieve any spiritual advancement by his own strength:

Wednesday, Jan. 2, 1722–23. Dull. I find, by experience, that, let me make resolutions, and do what I will, with never so many inventions, it is all nothing, and to no purpose at all, without the motions of the Spirit of God; for if the Spirit of God should be as much withdrawn from me always, as for the week past, notwithstanding all I do, I should not grow, but should languish, and miserably fade away. I perceive, if God should withdraw His Spirit a little more, I should not hesitate to break my resolutions, and should soon arrive at my old state. There is no dependence on myself.[7]

One week later, Edwards again admitted his weakness and inability to keep the resolutions he was making. The problem was his heart, which remained deceitful. Even when he made a "strong resolution," he had not the strength to keep it: "Wednesday, Jan. 9. At night. . . . How deceitful is my heart! I take up a strong resolution, but how soon doth it weaken!"[8] Edwards was becoming an expert in his own inability.

The same humbling realization struck again the next week. Edwards found he was too weak to do anything spiritually pleasing to God. He lamented: "Jan. 15, Tuesday. . . . But alas! How soon do I decay! O how weak, how infirm, how unable to do anything of myself! What a poor inconsistent being! What a miserable wretch, without the assistance of the Spirit of God. . . . How weak do I find myself! O let it teach me to depend less on myself, to be more humble."[9]

Later that winter, Edwards acknowledged the inability of even the elect to do anything of spiritual value apart from divine grace. He wrote: "Wednesday, Mar. 6, near sunset. Felt the doctrines of election, free grace, and of our not being able to do anything without the grace of God; and that holiness is entirely, throughout, the work of God's Spirit, with more pleasure than before."[10]

Edwards composed his "Resolutions" with a proper self-assessment. He understood that no matter how resolved or determined he might be, he could not glorify God in his own strength. It was one thing to make a resolution, but something else entirely to keep it. He saw that living the Christian life involved far more than merely selecting a path to pursue. He needed more.

## DIVINE ENABLEMENT

Coupled with Edwards' awareness of his weakness was the recognition that he needed God's power in order to keep his "Resolutions." The preamble continues: "I do humbly entreat him by his grace to enable me to keep these Resolutions." With these words, Edwards conceded that the experience of divine power in his pursuit of godliness was not automatic. He saw that he bore a real responsibility to "entreat" the Lord for sanctifying grace,[11] a testimony and pledge of his full dependence on God.[12]

George S. Claghorn writes, "Edwards depended on the sustaining strength of his omnipotent Deity to enable him to live up to [his Resolutions]."[13] Likewise, Nichols notes that Edwards began the "Resolutions" with "a humble acknowledgement of dependence on God."[14] Dwight writes:

> He [Edwards] therefore in the outset looked to God for aid, who alone can afford success in the use of the best means, and in the intended accomplishment of the best purposes. This he places at the head of all his other important rules that his whole dependence was on the grace of God, while he still proposes to recur to a frequent and serious perusal of them, in order that they might become the habitual directory of his life.[15]

Various entries in Edwards' diary express his desire to seek God for grace to walk in His ways. It was a reliance that he did not always find easy:

> Wednesday, Jan. 2. . . . Our resolutions may be at the highest one day, and yet, the next day, we may be in a miserable dead condition, not at all like the same person who resolved. So that it is to no purpose to resolve, except we depend on the grace of God.

For, if it were not for His mere grace, one might be a very good man one day, and a very wicked one the next.[16]

Jan. 15, Tuesday. . . . While I stand, I am ready to think that I stand by my own strength, and upon my own legs; and I am ready to triumph over my spiritual enemies, as if it were I myself that caused them to flee:—when alas! I am but a poor infant, upheld by Jesus Christ; who holds me up, and gives me liberty to smile to see my enemies flee, when He drives them before me. And so I laugh, as though I myself did it, when it is only Jesus Christ leads me along, and fights Himself against my enemies. . . . O let it teach me to depend less on myself, to be more humble, and to give more of the praise of my ability to Jesus Christ![17]

William S. Morris writes that Edwards was keenly aware of the danger of self-reliance in keeping his "Resolutions." He notes, "The search for personal holiness through self-discipline must not be allowed to blind one to the truth that only God's sovereign grace acting in and on the soul to strengthen and nourish it could enable the soul to possess that creature holiness for which it so much yearned."[18] By admitting his need for divine help, Edwards guarded against the subtle trap of dependence on his inadequate strength.

## HUMBLE SUBMISSION

Edwards knew he could not expect God to respond to his entreaties for help to keep his "Resolutions" unless they were, as he put it in the preamble, "agreeable to his will." In short, Edwards knew that God would not help him if he set out to do something that was contrary to God's desires. Thus, in drafting his vows, he purposed not to set forth his own agenda and expect God to bless it. Rather, the "Resolutions" must be a humble attempt to submit himself to the will of God in all things, for God's will *rules*.[19] God had charted a course for his life, one that was "good and acceptable and perfect" (Rom. 12:2), and he must submit to that divine plan in and through his "Resolutions."

Edwards recognized that submission to God's will necessitated being completely dedicated to God. As a result, he committed himself to strive after such complete surrender. Sam Storms writes: "Although profoundly heavenly minded, Jonathan Edwards was no less dedicated to a vibrant and fruitful life for God on the earth. He would never have considered using the former to justify laxity in the latter."[20]

Edwards described his consecration to God in a remarkable diary entry, which, George Marsden notes, "became a milestone in his spiritual autobiography":[21]

Saturday, Jan. 12 [1723]. In the morning. . . . I have been before God, and have given myself, all that I am and have, to God; so that I am not, in any respect, my own. I can challenge no right in this understanding, this will, these affections, which are in me. Neither have I any right to this body, or any of its members—no right to this tongue, these hands, these feet; no right to these senses, these eyes, these ears, this smell, or this taste. I have given myself clear away, and have not retained any thing as my own. . . . I have been this morning to Him, and told Him, that I gave myself wholly to him. I have given every power to Him; so that, for the future, I'll challenge no right in myself, in no respect whatever. . . . I have this morning told Him that I did take Him for my whole portion and felicity, looking on nothing else as any part of my happiness, nor acting as if it were; and [take] His law, for the constant rule of my obedience; and would fight with all my might against the world, the flesh, and the devil, to the end of my life; and that I did believe in Jesus Christ, and did receive Him as a Prince and Saviour; and that I would adhere to the faith and obedience of the gospel, however hazardous and difficult the confession and practice of it may be. [22]

In that same entry, Edwards declared that he had presented himself to God as a living sacrifice:

I pray God, for the sake of Christ, to look upon it as a self-dedication, and to receive me now as entirely His own, and to deal with me, in all respects, as such, whether He afflicts me or prospers me, or whatever He pleases to do with me, who am His. Now, henceforth, I am not to act, in any respect, as my own.—I shall act as my own, if I ever make use of any of my powers to any thing that is not to the glory of God, and do not make the glorifying of Him my whole and entire business:— if I murmur in the least at affliction; if I grieve at the prosperity of others; if I am in any way uncharitable; if I am angry because of injuries; if I revenge them; if I do any thing purely to please myself, or if I avoid any thing for the sake of my own ease; if I omit any thing because it is great self-denial; if I trust to myself; if I take any of the praise of the good that I do, or that God doth by me; or if I am in any way proud.[23]

Edwards clearly realized his life was not his own, but that he belonged entirely to God and, therefore, must live in surrender to Him. As David Vaughn writes: "He was determined to devote himself to God. Indeed, this is the key to understanding his power and life."[24] Edwards knew he could not make a resolution that was contrary to God's will and expect His aid to keep it. Rather, every resolution must be in accord with God's will.

## PUREST MOTIVE

Edwards wanted all that he did, as the preamble indicates, to be "for Christ's sake." In other words, he wanted the supreme majesty of Christ to be the driving force behind each resolution. In one way or another, all seventy vows must promote the Father's glory revealed in His Son, Jesus Christ. With these three words, Edwards stated the supreme motive behind the composition of the "Resolutions"—the honor of Jesus Christ.[25] As Nichols writes, Edwards believed "there is a center that gives shape and meaning to life and to the world, . . . [and] this center is Christ Himself."[26] Therefore, he notes, "The *Resolutions* . . . reveal Edwards' utmost determination to bring every area of his life under the Lordship of Christ."[27] *Everything* must flow from a passion to magnify the unrivaled honor of Christ.

Edwards longed to love, honor, and magnify Christ more fully and consistently. He wrote in his diary: "Dec. 22, Saturday. This day, revived by God's Holy Spirit; affected with the sense of the excellency of holiness; felt more exercise of love to Christ, than usual. Have, also, felt sensible repentance for sin, because it was committed against so merciful and good a God."[28] Two days later, Edwards was drawn again to the magnification of Christ: "Monday, Dec. 24. Higher thoughts than usual of the excellency of Christ and His kingdom."[29] Soon after, while recovering from illness in early 1723, Edwards wrote that he must not let himself become pre-occupied with temporal matters but remain focused in his love for the Savior: "Thursday, Jan. 10. 'Tis a great dishonour to Christ, in whom I hope I have an interest, to be uneasy at my worldly state and condition."[30]

Edwards believed that *all* things in his life were "for

Christ's sake." Every thought, passion, and desire must lead to the glory and honor of Christ. He knew he was not his own, but belonged to Christ. Therefore, he must decrease and Christ must increase, so he reveled in the advancement of Christ's kingdom. As he reflected in his "Personal Narrative":

> My heart has been much on the advancement of Christ's kingdom in the world. The histories of the past advancement of Christ's kingdom, have been sweet to me. When I have read histories of past ages, the pleasantest thing in all my reading has been, to read of the kingdom of Christ being promoted. And when I have expected in my reading, to come to any such thing, I have lotted upon it all the way as I read. And my mind has been much entertained and delighted, with the Scripture promises and prophecies, of the future glorious advancement of Christ's kingdom on earth.[31]

For Edwards, the advancement of the glory of God in Christ was *everything*.

## REGULAR REVIEW

Edwards believed that he must keep continually before him the spiritual goals he set out in his "Resolutions." Therefore, he closed the preamble with a brief exhortation to himself: "Remember to read over these Resolutions once a week." The

Puritans were known to submit themselves "to divine searching . . . to monitor their motives and actions."[32] Accordingly, Colonial believers practiced "introspection as a duty of great consequence."[33] True to his Puritan heritage, Edwards determined that he "would read each of [the resolutions] aloud once a week for the rest of his life"[34] as scheduled maintenance for his inner man.[35]

Shortsightedness was not in Edwards' vocabulary. The composition of the "Resolutions" was by no means a passing impulse. Instead, when Edwards wrote them, he purposed to keep them until he drew his last breath. As Nichols writes, "Throughout his life, the *Resolutions* were his constant companion."[36] John Gerstner concurs, noting that the "Resolutions" "were conscientiously carried out in practice the rest of his life."[37] Edwards did this by regularly reading over the "Resolutions" in order to gauge his spiritual progress. He wrote in his diary:

> Monday, Dec. 24. . . . Concluded to observe, at the end of every month, the number of breaches of resolutions, to see whether they increase or diminish, to begin from this day, and to compute from that the weekly account, my monthly increase, and out of the whole, my yearly increase, beginning from new-year days.[38]

In Edwards' estimation, such constant examination of his soul was essential if he was to grow in grace. He even attempted to review his progress in keeping his "Resolutions" while busy with other matters: "Tuesday morning, June 18. *Memorandum.* To do this part, which I conveniently can, of my stated exercise, while about other business, such as self-examination, resolutions, &c. that I may do the remainder in less time."[40]

## THE CALL FOR COMMITMENT

Every believer today stands exactly where Edwards stood so long ago. Human inability to please God has not changed in the least over the past three centuries. All Christians remain in constant need of divine grace to enable them to pursue holiness. This requires, as it did for Edwards, humble submission and dedication to God, all for the honor of Christ. Only in such self-denial is divine grace multiplied in one's life.

If one is to impact this world for Jesus Christ, he must live as Edwards did, with extraordinary purpose and firm determination. God is looking for individuals in this generation who will rise above the status quo of contemporary Christianity and say with Edwards, "I am completely Yours." God is searching for those people in this hour who will strive to be that one in this generation who is the most complete Christian.

May God bring you to this place of submission to Christ. May you present your body as a living sacrifice to Him. May you not be conformed to this world, but be renewed in your mind. Only then will you prove what is the will of God, that which is good and acceptable and perfect.

This is what Edwards found. How can we settle for less?

## Notes

1. John DeWitt, "Jonathan Edwards: A Study," *Biblical and Theological Studies* (Birmingham, Ala.: Solid Ground Christian Books, 1912, 2003), 126.
2. Curt Daniel, *The History and Theology of Calvinism* (Dallas, Texas: Scholarly Reprints, 1993), 99.
3. Sereno E. Dwight, "Memoir," in Jonathan Edwards," *The Works of Jonathan Edwards, Vol. 1* (Edinburgh: Banner of Truth Trust, 1974), xx.
4. Stephen Nichols, *Jonathan Edwards' Resolutions and Advice to Young Converts* (Phillipsburg, N.J.: P&R, 2001), 10.
5. This truth of the believer's weakness is taught in various passages: John 15:5; Romans 7:15–23; 2 Corinthians 3:5a; 12:9–10; and Galatians 3:3; 5:17.
6. Dwight, "Memoir," in Edwards, *Works, Vol. 1*, xx.
7. Jonathan Edwards, "Diary," *The Works of Jonathan Edwards, Vol. 16, Letters and Personal Writings*, ed. George S. Claghorn (New Haven, Conn.: Yale University Press, 1998), 760.
8. Ibid., 761.
9. Ibid., 764–765.
10. Ibid., 767.
11. The reality that the believer must petition God to empower him in fulfilling the duties of the Christian life is taught in Ephesians 1:18–23; 3:20–21; and Colossians 1:9–11.
12. This truth of the sufficiency of God's inward power, enabling the believer to live the Christian life in a manner that pleases God, is taught in John 15:4–5; Acts 1:8; 1 Corinthians 12:6; 15:10; 2 Corinthians 2:14; 3:5; 12:9–10; Ephesians 3:20–21; 5:18; Philippians 1:6; 2:13; and Colossians 1:29.
13. George S. Claghorn, "Introduction," in Edwards, *Works* (Yale), *Vol. 16*, 741.
14. Stephen Nichols, *Jonathan Edwards: A Guided Tour of His Life and Thoughts* (Phillipsburg, N.J.: P&R, 2001), 38.

15. Dwight, "Memoir," in Edwards, *Works, Vol. 1*, xx.

16. Edwards, "Diary," *Works* (Yale), *Vol. 16*, 760.

17. Ibid., 764.

18. William S. Morris, *The Young Jonathan Edwards: A Reconstruction* (Eugene, Ore.: Wipf & Stock, 2005), 44.

19. This foundational truth is taught in Scripture in multiple places: Psalm 40:8; Matthew 6:10; 26:39–42; Luke 22:42; John 4:34; 5:30; 6:38; Acts 21:14; Romans 12:1–2; and Colossians 1:9.

20. Sam Storms, *Signs of the Spirit: An Interpretation of Jonathan Edwards' Religious Affections* (Wheaton, Ill.: Crossway, 2007), 182.

21. George Marsden, *Jonathan Edwards: A Life* (New Haven, Conn./London: Yale University Press, 2003), 53.

22. Edwards, "Diary," *Works* (Yale), *Vol. 16*, 762.

23. Ibid.

24. David Vaughn, *A Divine Light: The Spiritual Leadership of Jonathan Edwards* (Nashville: Cumberland House, 2007), 32.

25. This emphasis upon pursuing the glory of Christ in all things is asserted throughout Scripture: Matthew 17:5; John 5:23; 13:31–32; Romans 1:4–5; 1 Corinthians 15:28; Philippians 2:9–11; and Colossians 1:18.

26. Nichols, *Jonathan Edwards: A Guided Tour of His Life and Thought*, 156.

27. Nichols, *Jonathan Edwards' Resolutions*, 10.

28. Edwards, "Diary," *Works,* (Yale), *Vol. 16,* 759.

29. Ibid., 760.

30. Ibid., 761.

31. Edwards, "Personal Narrative," *Works* (Yale), *Vol. 16,* 800.

32. Claghorn, "Introduction," in Edwards, *Works* (Yale), *Volume 16,* 741.

33. Ibid.

34. Daniel, *The History and Theology of Calvinism*, 99.

35. This principle of self-examination by the believer is taught in the following passages: Psalm 17:3; 26:2; 139:23–24; Proverbs 4:23; 1 Corinthians 11:28; 2 Corinthians 13:5; and Galatians 6:4.

36. Nichols, *Jonathan Edwards' Resolutions*, 11.

37. John H. Gerstner, *The Rational Biblical Theology of Jonathan Edwards, Vol. 1* (Powhatan, Va.: Berea Publications, 1991), 13.

38. Edwards, "Diary," *Works* (Yale), *Vol. 16,* 760.

39. Ibid., 772.

# CHAPTER FOUR

# The Priority of God's Glory

*Common to all of Edwards's theology and piety was a passion for God's glory. . . . Edwards carefully and logically defended the position that God's ultimate purpose is to glorify himself in all his works.*[1]

—JAMES MONTGOMERY BOICE

Every great Christian leader has a master passion, an overruling ambition that dominates his life and drives his soul. It is that in which he most believes, that which most captures his mind and enflames his heart. Such a chief aim controls him and defines his very reason for being. This supreme sense of purpose becomes a motivation so strong that it empowers him to overcome all obstacles and override all adversity. For Jonathan Edwards, this passion was the *summum bonum* set forth in Scripture, the highest good in the universe—the glory of God.

Edwards believed that God's ultimate end in all things is the manifestation of His glory. In his theological masterpiece, *Dissertation on the End for Which God Created the World*, penned near the end of his life (1755), he argued that God made the world for His own glory. "For it appears that all that is ever spoken of in the Scripture as an ultimate end of God's works," Edwards stated, "is included in that one phrase, the glory of God."[2] That being the case, Edwards concluded that bringing glory to God must be his preeminent purpose. This pursuit was firmly established in him from the very beginning of his Christian walk.

When Edwards traveled to New York City to be the interim pastor of the First Presbyterian Church in August 1722, he was full of passion to serve God. In his "Personal Narrative," an autobiographical work penned years later (1740), Edwards wrote: "My longings after God and holiness, were much increased. Pure and humble, holy and heavenly Christianity appeared exceeding amiable to me. I felt in me a burning desire to be in everything a complete Christian."[3]

In the fall of 1722, Edwards began to channel that passion through his "Resolutions," expecting that they would "guide him in living the Christian life."[4] As the "Resolutions" reveal, Edwards had become remarkably single-minded, indeed riveted, on the pursuit of the glory of God, and the "Resolutions" were the instrument by which he hoped to govern his life to this highest end.

This chapter will examine the resolutions in which Edwards focused on God's glory, numbers 1, 2, 4, 23, and 27. In them we see five aspects of his Christian walk.

## CHIEF AMBITION

The first resolution sets the tone for all that follow. In this statement, Edwards declared that the glory of God would be his chief aim and the factor that would guide all his actions and decisions. Edwards wrote:

> 1. Resolved, that I will do whatsoever I think to be most to God's glory, and my own good, profit and pleasure, in the whole of my duration, without any consideration of the time, whether now, or never so many myriads of ages hence. Resolved to do whatever I think to be my duty, and most for the good and advantage of mankind in general. Resolved to do this, whatever difficulties I meet with, how many and how great soever.

The word *resolved* appears at the beginning of this resolution and virtually all of the resolutions that follow. Sixty-six of the seventy resolutions start with *resolved*; only in the last one is it not found. In this first resolution, the word *resolved* occurs three times, emphasizing Edwards' firm spiritual purpose. To be resolved is "to be fixed, settled, fully determined, deliberate, decided."[5] In short, the "Resolutions" were "fixed determinations."[6] Edwards had made up his mind that he would live with unwavering deliberation to promote God's glory.

Edwards first purposed, "I will do whatsoever I think to be

most to God's glory." As many tributaries flow into one raging torrent, so Edwards wanted every current of his life to feed into this one rushing river, his pursuit of God's glory. All his aims, ambitions, and activities must be channeled into exalting and extolling his Creator. This initial resolution, of course, flowed down directly from the lofty peaks of his God-centered theology.

Commenting on Edwards' chief aim, Sereno E. Dwight writes: "The glory of God was his supreme object, whether engaged in his devotional exercises, his studies, his social intercourse, the discharge of his public ministry, or in the publication of his writings. All inferior motives seem to have been without any discernible influence upon him."[7] Dwight further states: "[Edwards] set the Lord always before him; encouraging upon all occasions an earnest concern for the glory of God, the grand object for which he desired to live both upon earth and in heaven, an object compared with which all other things seemed in his view but trifles."[8]

What is more, Edwards affirmed in his first resolution that prioritizing God's glory would be to "my own good, profit and pleasure." In other words, Edwards believed that prizing God above all else would lead to his greatest benefit. These two ends—God's glory and his good—were not in competition, but were complementary. As David Vaughn explains, "The glory of God and the happiness of man are not two ultimate ends; rather, these two ends are one."[9] Dwight writes that Edwards' emotional state was inseparably linked with his pursuit of the glory of God: "If this were attained, all his desires

66

were satisfied; but if this were lost or imperfectly gained, his soul was filled with anguish."[10]

The more Edwards sought God's glory, the more he found his deepest happiness. When he asked himself "whether any delight or satisfaction ought to be allowed . . . besides a religious one,"[11] Edwards' answered in the affirmative, for rejoicing in God allowed him to enjoy all things lawful in life: "Saturday, Jan. 12. . . . I answer, Yes, because, if we should never suffer ourselves to rejoice, but because we have obtained a religious end, we should never rejoice at the sight of friends, we should not allow ourselves any pleasure in our food, whereby the animal spirits would be withdrawn, and good digestion hindered. But the query is to be answered thus—We never ought to allow any joy or sorrow, but what helps religion."[12] With this stance, Edwards declared that his joy was linked to advancing God's glory.

As Edwards embraced God as his greatest pleasure, he displayed the Puritan mindset. Such a joy-saturated life admittedly goes against modern stereotypes, which depict the Puritans as harsh and cold. But as Stephen Holmes correctly notes: "These Calvinists were more optimistic and life-affirming than most. They believed in a God who was totally committed to His people, who had created this world as the perfect place for them, and who still promised eternal joy and pleasures at His right hand."[13] This was certainly true of Edwards.

Continuing on, Edwards wrote, "Resolved to do whatever I think to be my duty, and most for the good and advantage of mankind in general." Edwards was committed to fulfilling his "duty" to live out the biblical commands to love his neighbor in tangible ways. He knew that a vertical focus on God's glory yielded a horizontal focus on the good of other people. In other words, loving his neighbor was a significant way to bring glory to God. The pursuit of the glory of God and the good of mankind, Edwards believed, were indivisibly bound together.

Edwards was careful to note that he must render service to others in a selfless way, with no thought for the honor he might gain from it: "Saturday night, May 18. . . . I think it the best way, in general, not to seek for honour, in any other way, than by seeking to be good and to do good. I may pursue knowledge, religion, the glory of God, and the good of mankind with the utmost vigour; but am to leave the honour of it entirely at God's disposal, as a thing with which I have no immediate concern."[14] Such selfless living was a means of glorifying God.

Finally, Edwards realized that living for the glory of God would never be easy. So he concluded his first resolution with these words: "Resolved to do this, whatever difficulties I meet with, how many and how great soever." By this, Edwards meant he would pursue God's glory no matter what the cost. Even through persecution and poverty, Edwards was determined to uphold the glory of God in his life.

Even as a young man, Edwards faced many difficulties, and he admitted that they were often discouraging. But he learned to view his trials as blessings sent from God to advance his growth in holiness. He made up his mind to give his cares and concerns to God, thereby glorifying Him: "Tuesday afternoon, July 23. . . . To improve afflictions, of all kinds, as blessed opportunities of forcibly bearing on, in my Christian course, notwithstanding that which is so very apt to discourage me, and to damp the vigour of my mind, and to make me lifeless . . . let me comfort myself, that 'tis the very nature of afflictions, to make the heart better; and, if I am made better by them, what need I be concerned, however grievous they seem for the present?"[15] In other words, Edwards came to believe that greater trouble brings greater triumph.

He noted that even Christ's glory was enhanced through His suffering: "Wednesday forenoon, Aug. 7. . . . Religion is the sweeter, and what is gained by labour is abundantly more precious, as a woman loves her child the more for having brought it forth with travail; and even to Christ Jesus Himself, His mediatorial glory, His victory and triumph, the kingdom which He hath obtained, how much more glorious is it, how much more excellent and precious, for His having wrought it out with such agonies."[16] Edwards would see the truth of this statement in his life.

## Relentless Pursuit

The second resolution built upon the first, as Edwards continued to focus on the glory of God. He wrote:

2. Resolved, to be continually endeavoring to find out some new invention and contrivance to promote the forementioned things.

By this vow, Edwards purposed to seek continuously for new ways to "promote" the realization of the goal laid out in the first resolution—the glory of God. He feared he might fall into the rut that leads to mediocrity in Christian living. Thus, he pledged to look constantly for "some new invention and contrivance" that would extol God.

What did Edwards have in mind here? It might be a new venue for preaching the Word or a new way to promote corporate prayer. It might be a new manner in which to conduct his personal devotions, a new place to be alone with God, or a new ministry to undertake. Edwards simply wanted to discover every means at his disposal to promote God's glory.

One of the heart cries of the Reformation was *semper reformanda*, meaning "always reforming.'" That is, believers must be constantly seeking to conform what they believe and how they live more closely to the unchanging standard of God's Word. By this resolution, Edwards sought to be always reforming his life for better pursuit of the glory of God.

## COMPREHENSIVE STRATEGY

In the fourth resolution, Edwards pledged that his pursuit of God's glory would be comprehensive. No area of his life would be compartmentalized and detached from this chief aim:

> 4. Resolved, never to do any manner of thing, whether in soul or body, less or more, but what tends to the glory of God; nor be, nor suffer it, if I can avoid it.

With this resolution, Edwards vowed he would never do what failed to promote the glory of God. This "doing" would encompass *all* the actions of the soul, such as thoughts, affections, and choices, as well as those of the body, which referred to all his activities. Whether an internal attitude or external act, all things ("less or more") must be for God's glory. The determinative factor in every endeavor would be to choose that which most promoted the divine honor.

Edwards *did* continually pursue God's glory in every arena of life, as the conclusion of his long pastorate in Northampton, Massachusetts, attests. Near the end of his time at the church (1728–1750), he came to the conviction that those who would come to the Lord's Table must first profess Christ and live in a worthy manner. This was a marked departure from the teaching of his grandfather and predecessor, Solomon Stoddard, who saw the Lord's Supper as a converting ordinance. As a result of that stance, Edwards received considerable opposition from his flock, but he was more concerned with pleasing God than men. Tragically, his Northampton congregation dismissed him as their pastor, rejecting the man who, along with George Whitefield, had been the leader of the Great Awakening.

After he was expelled, Edwards could have gone to Scotland or to prominent places in the Colonies. Instead, he made a difficult decision to minister on an elementary level to Native Americans on the Colonial frontier in Stockbridge. One of the greatest thinkers in American history willingly communicated the gospel on a simple level because he believed that would most glorify God.

## INTENTIONAL ENDEAVOR

Edwards further resolved to do things that seemed unlikely to be done for God's glory. In resolution 23, he wrote:

> 23. Resolved, frequently to take some deliberate action, which seems most unlikely to be done, for the glory of God, and trace it back to the original intention, designs and ends of it; and if I find it not to be for God's glory, to repute it as a breach of the 4th Resolution.

This resolution was a vow to pursue ways to promote God's honor that he judged himself "most unlikely" to undertake. In other words, he wanted to do that which was most challenging and, at times, unnatural to his own sinful inclinations. He knew he must not take the path of least resistance, but pursue those tasks that required the greatest sacrifice on his part. It might be a new outreach with the gospel, a new study of the Word, or a new avenue of serving others. Edwards set himself to take such actions "frequently." He also specified that any such action must be "deliberate," a word that conveys how intentional he sought to be in promoting God's glory. He would carefully consider a difficult action and then undertake it.

Edwards also resolved that, having taken an "unlikely" action, he would evaluate it. First, he felt he must "trace back" all that he did to the "original intention." This was his heart motive, which must be pure; it must be to the praise and honor of God, not for the promotion of himself. Second, he must examine his "designs," or the practical means he chose to carry out the action. These must be consistent with Scripture's teaching about honoring God. If the motive was right but the method was wrong, God would be defamed. Third, the "ends" must be those that most honored God.

If Edwards' evaluation found that his intention, designs, and aims were not motivated and molded by God's glory, he pledged that he would "repute" his effort as a violation of his fourth resolution. That is, he would repent of and reject any action that did not truly promote God's glory. The *why*, the *how*, and the *what* must be in order if Edwards was to hit the mark.

## PURPOSEFUL OMISSIONS

In resolution 27, Edwards purposed to do whatever he believed to be the will of God. To neglect any God-given responsibility

73

would be to sin against God Himself—unless the omission would be the proper course:

> 27. Resolved, never willfully to omit anything, except the omission be for the glory of God; and frequently to examine my omissions.

As Edwards examined his life, he faced the difficult decision of what to omit. There was always much to do, and the demands on his life mounted when he became the pastor of the Northampton congregation. There were sermons to write, parishioners to shepherd, visits to make, individuals to counsel, letters to write, prayers to offer, books to read, and much more. Edwards quickly discovered no man can do everything. How could he navigate the maze? What would he omit?

Edwards determined that he must do those things that would glorify God, but he would omit every matter that did not tend so strongly to the magnification of God's honor. In other words, he passed up the *good* and the *better* for the *best*. He could only afford time to do that which chiefly promoted the honor of God's name. But because these choices were so important, he purposed "frequently to examine my omissions." He wanted to be certain he was removing from his life those things that brought the least glory to God.

# How Will You Live?

Edwards possessed a burning commitment to God's glory that permeated everything he did, said, and wrote, and overshadowed every competing ambition. This became his controlling passion and consuming desire. The God of glory had captured his heart.

Living for God's honor must be the chief aim in every person's life. But what brings the most glory to God? This is the interpretive key for every life decision. Do you want to know God's will for your life? Do you want to know who to marry? Do you want to know what job to take? Do you want to know what ministry you should pursue? Do you want to know how to invest your resources? Do you want to know how to spend your time or how to use your tongue? Every decision and direction must come under this overarching goal of bringing glory to God.

A life of resolve comes with a price tag. You will be tested by the lure of the world. But you must turn a deaf ear to the crowd and live instead for the approbation of Christ. There will always be a cross before a crown, sacrifice before success, and reproach before a reward. The call of discipleship will cost you popularity, possessions, and position. But God will use your commitment. The grace of God will be multiplied in you if you cultivate a fixed resolution to live for the glory of God.

May you not settle for living for what is merely *good*. May you pursue what is *best*—the glory of God in all things.

## Notes

1. James Montgomery Boice and Philip Graham Ryken, *The Doctrines of Grace* (Wheaton, Ill.: Crossway, 2002), 49.
2. Jonathan Edwards, "Dissertation on the End for Which God Created the World," *The Works of Jonathan Edwards, Vol. I* (Edinburgh: Banner of Truth Trust, 1834, 1979), 119.
3. Jonathan Edwards, "Personal Narrative," *The Works of Jonathan Edwards, Vol. 16, Letters and Personal Writings*, ed. George S. Claghorn (New Haven, Conn.: Yale University Press, 1998), 795.
4. Philip F. Gura, *Jonathan Edwards: America's Evangelical* (New York: Hill and Wang, 2005), 31.
5. *The New Shorter Oxford English Dictionary* (Oxford/New York: Oxford University Press, 1933, 1993), II, 2563–2564.
6. Claghorn, "Introduction," *Works* (Yale), *Vol. 16*, 741.
7. Sereno E. Dwight, "Memoir," in Edwards, *The Works of Jonathan Edwards, Vol. I*, xi.
8. Ibid., xxiii.
9. David Vaughn, *A Divine Light: The Spiritual Leadership of Jonathan Edwards* (Nashville: Cumberland House, 2007), 203.
10. Dwight, "Memoir," *Works, Vol. I*, xxiii.
11. Edwards, "Diary," *Works* (Yale), *Vol. 16*, 763.
12. Ibid.
13. Stephen R. Holmes, *God of Grace and God of Glory: An Account of the Theology of Jonathan Edwards* (Grand Rapids: Eerdmans, 2000, 2001), 12.
14. Edwards, "Diary," *Works* (Yale), *Vol. 16*, 770.
15. Ibid., 775–776.
16. Ibid., 778.

# CHAPTER FIVE

# The Putting Away of Sin

*Edwards's spirituality exhibited itself not only in a deep humility but also in a profound holiness. All who knew him were impressed with his integrity, honesty, fairness, and modesty, all of which were rooted in his soul's conformity to the will of God.*[1]

—DAVID VAUGHAN

S in is the antithesis of God's glory, a contradiction of His holy nature. It is all that falls short of God's blameless character, amounting to nothing less than cosmic treason against the Creator. Jonathan Edwards understood this. What is more, he was persuaded of the inward polluting power of sin. Edwards knew that if he was to glorify God, he must resist sin with all his might, and deal with it decisively and radically.

Edwards stood in the Reformed theological tradition, which taught him that he would face an ongoing internal conflict against sin throughout his life. As George Marsden writes, "His Calvinist framework itself demanded that even the greatest saints acknowledge their ongoing sinfulness."[2] Given his determination to glorify God, and his understanding that sin was an impediment to that goal, Edwards resolved that he would struggle fiercely against his sin as long as he lived.

In *Jonathan Edwards: A New Biography*, Iain H. Murray titled one chapter "New York: The Pursuit of Holiness," capturing the thrust of Edwards' life during the time when he wrote his "Resolutions." It was a season in which "a new master-interest possessed him,"[3] when a new "all-absorbing interest"[4] came into his life. This "new prevailing bent of Edwards' mind and heart"[5] was the result of regeneration, which gave him a new desire for holiness. But Edwards soon found that the realization of that desire was an "immense struggle."[6] Marsden writes, "Despite his massive intellect and heroic disciplines, he was, like everyone else, a person with frailties and contradictions."[7]

In his "Personal Narrative," Edwards reflected upon the beauty of holiness that he sought to attain: "Holiness . . . appeared to me to be of sweet, pleasant, charming, serene, calm nature. It seemed to me, it brought an inexpressible purity, brightness, peacefulness and ravishment to the soul."[8] Edwards wrote that holiness transformed his inner man, making it increasingly "all pleasant, delightful and undisturbed."[9] This growth in grace allowed him to enjoy "a sweet calm, and the gently vivifying beams of the sun."[10] His was the soul of a true Christian, enjoying holiness but fighting sin.

This chapter focuses on Edwards' desire to put away sin. Resolutions 3, 8, 24, 37, 56, and 68 are among those that deal with this issue. In these pledges, we see Edwards' commitment to resist and root out sin from his life.

## GENUINE REPENTANCE

In his Christian life, Edwards resolved to give himself to an ongoing lifestyle of repentance. The word *repentance* means a change of mind, but as it is used in Scripture, it includes the concept of a change of heart and will. The result of these changes is a new life direction. Repentance involves turning away from sin with godly sorrow, confessing it as sin, and turning to God for the pursuit of holiness. In short, repentance is a 180-degree change of direction—and a 170-degree change is not acceptable. In his third resolution, Edwards purposed to repent whenever he found that he had failed to keep one of his resolutions. He wrote:

> 3. Resolved, if ever I shall fall and grow dull, so as to neglect to keep any part of these Resolutions, to repent of all I can remember, when I come to myself again.

Even as he wrote the "Resolutions," Edwards was concerned that he would unknowingly violate them. Therefore, he established a procedure to follow when he should "come to [himself] again," that is, when he should realize how he had failed. He would search his memory and repent of the failure as thoroughly as possible.

Of course, Edwards was concerned to deal with all sin in his life, not just violations of the "Resolutions." His writings indicate that whenever he became aware of *any* sin, he sought to turn away from it. With his mind, he would concur with God about the evil of this sin in his life. Then, with his heart, he would grieve over such sin. Finally, with his will, he would choose to remove it from his life.

As Edwards' diary entry of May 4, 1723, indicates, he understood repentance to necessitate "amending" his sinful ways. He realized he must alter the course of his life away from particular sins: "Saturday night, May 4. O that God would help me to discover all the flaws and defects of my temper and conversation, and help me in the difficult work of amending them; and that he would grant me so full a measure of vital Christianity, that the foundation of all those disagreeable irregularities may be destroyed, and the contrary sweetnesses and beauties may of themselves naturally follow."[11]

All "flaws and defects," he wrote, must be decisively addressed and corrected. This included turning from sin involving his inward "temper" and outward "conversation." Such repentance was difficult and demanding work, and required God's gracious "help." Edwards saw that the Lord Himself must grant the ability to repent. Only when his sins, what he called "disagreeable irregularities," were removed would the "sweetnesses and beauties" of holiness come.

## GODLY SORROW

Edwards understood that true repentance must be accompanied by godly sorrow. In resolution 8, he wrote:

> 8. Resolved, to act, in all respects, both speaking and doing, as if nobody had been so vile as I, and as if I had committed the same sins, or had the same infirmities or failings as others; and that I will let the knowledge of their failings promote nothing but shame in myself, and prove only an occasion of my confessing my own sins and misery to God.

Whenever Edwards saw sin in another person, he took inventory on his own soul to search for the same iniquity. He was deeply concerned that his observations of sins in others might produce pride in his heart. Thus, he pledged to regard himself as the most sinful person alive and as if he had committed all the sins, or faced the same temptations, as those whose transgressions he observed. When he saw sin in others, he wanted it to prompt him to feel shame over his own wrongdoing and to drive him to confess it to God.

As a new Christian, Edwards came to realize he was often self-deceived about his spiritual progress. He admitted in his diary that he often wrongly assumed he was doing better than he actually was: "Wednesday, Jan. 9. At night . . . I am sometimes apt to think, that I have a great deal more of holiness than I really have."[12]

Recognizing this self-delusion, Edwards examined his own thoughts, attitudes, and affections, often finding much deceit: "Jan. 20, Sabbath day. At night. . . . I find my heart so deceitful, that I am almost discouraged from making any more resolutions. Wherein have I been negligent in the week past; and how could I have done better, to help the dreadful, low estate in which I am sunk?"[13]

Far worse, Edwards saw the pollution of pride in his heart. His desire for humility before the Lord was constantly opposed by self-exalting arrogance. This tendency troubled him greatly: "Saturday, Mar. 2. O how much more base and vile am I, when I feel pride working in me. . . . How hateful is a proud man! How hateful is a worm that lifts up itself with pride! What a foolish, silly, miserable, blind, deceived, poor worm am I, when pride works!"[14] He touched on the same theme in his "Personal Narrative," where he confessed: "I am greatly afflicted with a proud and self-righteous spirit; much more sensibly. . . . I see that serpent rising and putting forth its head, continually, everywhere, all around me."[15]

Edwards' soul-searching yielded a heightened sense of his sinfulness. He wrote: "I have had a vastly greater sense of my own wickedness, and the badness of my heart, since my conversion, than ever I had before. It has often appeared to me, that if God should mark iniquity against me, I should appear the very worst of all mankind; of all that have been since the beginning of the world to this time: and that I should have by far the lowest place in hell."[16]

He also marveled that he could have been so blind to his evil ways for so long: "It is affecting to me to think, how ignorant I was, when I was a young Christian, of the bottomless, infinite depths of wickedness, pride, hypocrisy and deceit left in my heart."[17]

As Edwards looked within, he often lamented over his fickle heart. In his words, he felt he should "bewail" his sin. In his diary, Edwards wrote: "January 21, Monday. . . . I ought to have spent the time in bewailing my sins, and in singing psalms, especially psalms or hymns of repentance; these duties being most suited to the frame I was in. I do not spend time enough in endeavouring to affect myself with the glories of Christianity."[18]

Edwards went yet further. Not only did he feel he ought to loathe his sin, he stated that his sin was sufficient cause for him to "abhor" himself. The ugliness of his sin nature was repulsive to him: "Monday afternoon, July 23. . . . To improve them, also, as opportunities to repent of and bewail my sin, and abhor myself; and as a blessed opportunity to exercise patience, to trust in God, and divest my mind from the affliction, by fixing myself in religious exercise."[19] These expressions reveal evidences of the godly sorrow Edwards sought in repentance. How could he be insensitive to that which grieves the heart of God?

## HEART INVESTIGATION

Putting away sin, for Edwards, meant tracing it back to the original motives. So Edwards determined in resolution 24 to backtrack until he had arrived at the "original cause" of his sin:

> 24. Resolved, whenever I do any conspicuously evil action, to trace it back, till I come to the original cause; and then both carefully endeavor to do so no more, and to fight and pray with all my might against the original of it.

Edwards had no illusions of sinlessness in this life. He knew regeneration had not removed his sin. Though he had embarked upon a new direction in life with new desires, the actual practice of righteousness was not always present. Consequently, this resolution begins, "*Whenever* I do any conspicuously evil action"—not "*if.*"

When he discovered sin in his life, Edwards felt compelled to trace it to its origin—the heart. Mere behavior modification was not enough for Edwards. A veneer of religiosity would only mask the real problem—the inner rotting of his heart. In order to become holy, he must trace the waters of sin upstream until he reached the springs from which his iniquity flowed—his motives. He wrote:

> Tuesday night, July 30. Have concluded to endeavour to work myself into duties by searching and tracing

back all the real reasons why I do them not, and narrowly searching out all the subtle subterfuges of my thoughts, and answering them to the utmost of my power, that I may know what are the very first originals of my defect, as with respect to want of repentance, love to God, loathing of myself,—to do this sometimes in sermons.[20]

As resolution 24 and the diary entry cited above show, Edwards believed that repentance is difficult and demanding. He knew he must "fight and pray with all my might" in order to correct the evil motives that prompted his sin. That was wholehearted effort; as he put it in his diary, the fight required "the utmost of my power." Nonchalant repentance is *no* repentance.

## Unyielding Fight

Though the fight against his sin was taxing and discouraging, Edwards knew he could not afford to rest on his laurels. In resolution 56, therefore, Edwards purposed that he would never slacken his efforts in the fight, no matter how many defeats he suffered:

56. Resolved, never to give over, nor in the least to slacken my fight with my corruptions, however unsuccessful I may be.

Edwards here committed himself to battling the corruptions he discovered in his life. He was on an unending mission to put his sin to death. He wrote: "Monday, Jan. 14. At night. Great instances of mortification are deep wounds given to the body of sin; hard blows, which make him stagger and reel. . . . After the greatest mortifications, I always find the greatest comfort."[21]

It was as if Edwards saw his battle with the old man as a life-or-death fight. This was no time for shadow boxing. Likewise, small blows would not suffice. To the contrary, he must inflict "deep wounds" and deliver hard body shots that would make his flesh "stagger and reel." He must go for a knockout in each round. He must beat the old man to the ground, and then hit him while he was down.

Edwards' battle surely included youthful lusts. Marsden writes, "His fretful disposition plus his pride and the resultant attitude toward others were the sins he combated most openly, but we can be sure that he was also fighting sexual desires, even if he did not directly record his struggles with those temptations."[22] Marsden notes that one possible allusion to such enticements is in a diary entry recorded on a Saturday night in July: "Saturday forenoon, July 27. When I am violently beset with temptation, or cannot rid myself of evil thoughts, to do some sum in arithmetic, or geometry, or some other study, which necessarily engages all my thoughts, and unavoidably keeps them from wandering."[23]

As he gained experience in the fight, Edwards saw that

triumph came through rigorous discipline. Edwards wrote: "Tuesday afternoon, July 23. . . . To count it all joy, when I have occasions of great self-denial; because, then, I have a glorious opportunity of giving deadly wounds to the body of sin, and of greatly confirming and establishing the new creature. I seek to mortify sin, and increase in holiness."[24]

But Edwards also realized he lacked the strength to overcome indwelling sin. His inward corruptions must be defeated in the power of God. Only the Holy Spirit can enable the believer to successfully overcome and mortify sin: "Saturday evening, Jan. 5. . . . Sin is not enough mortified. Without the influences of the Spirit of God, the old serpent would begin to rouse himself from his frozen state, and would come to life again."[25] Divine help was *essential* in the fight against sin.

## FULL CONFESSION

Edwards was determined to be brutally honest about his sin. In resolution 68, he pledged that whenever his investigations of his heart found sin, he would confess it to himself and to God:

> 68. Resolved, to confess frankly to myself all that which I find in myself, either infirmity or sin; and, if it be what concerns religion, also to confess the whole case to God, and implore needed help. July 23 and Aug. 10, 1723.

Edwards believed that true repentance involved bringing sin out into the open. He must not cover it up, downplay it, or turn a blind eye to it. He despised the temptation to shift blame, argue innocence, or wink at sin. He must not live in denial about his moral failure. Rather, he must acknowledge himself to be a sinner, justly deserving God's wrath and displeasure, then confess his transgressions to God in order to seek His forgiveness. Confession of sin is agreeing with God about one's sin. It is acknowledging sin to God for what it is—cosmic rebellion against a holy God.

Edwards felt that by confessing the sin he saw in his life, he would be enabled to go even deeper in tracing the roots of evil in his heart. In a restatement of resolution 68 in his diary, he wrote:

Saturday morning, Aug. 10. . . . As a help against that inward shameful hypocrisy, to confess frankly to myself all that which I find in myself, either infirmity or sin; also to confess to God, and open the whole case to Him, when it is what concerns religion, and humbly and earnestly implore of Him the help that is needed; not in the least to endeavour to smother what is in my heart, but to bring it all out to God and my conscience. By this means, I may arrive at a greater knowledge of my own heart.[26]

In a striking passage from his "Personal Narrative," Edwards expressed his keen sense of the depth of his sinfulness: "My wickedness, as I am in myself, has long appeared to me perfectly ineffable, and infinitely swallowing up all thought and imagination; like an infinite deluge, or infinite mountains over my head. I know not how to express better, what my sins appear to me to be, than by heaping infinite upon infinite, and multiplying infinite by infinite. . . . When I look into my heart and take a view of my wickedness, it looks like an abyss infinitely deeper than hell."[27] Edwards knew there *always* would be sin to confess to God. As long as he was alive, he would need to confess his iniquities.

## THE PURSUIT OF PERSONAL HOLINESS

Every believer who would pursue holiness engages in the fight against sin. Sanctification is an ongoing war with the world, the flesh, and the Devil to gain the high ground of godliness. It demands wholehearted commitment from every Christian soldier. Victory will never come if you do not wage war on the battlefield of your heart. Edwards fought as a tireless warrior in the fight against sin, and thus provides great inspiration for all who would follow his example.

The Christian must bring his sinful flesh into subjection to the Lord. In the battle with sin, common to all believers, sin must be refused, even put to death, through the power of the Holy Spirit. Meanwhile, we must seek to grow in Christlikeness. Like Nehemiah, we must fight with a sword in one hand and build with a trowel in the other. We must resist temptation and mortify sin, and at the same time we must grow in faith and fortify the new man. Both are necessary in realizing the overall goal of holiness.

May such a desire for personal holiness become your passion. Pursue the path of holiness by searching out your sin and confessing it to God in true repentance. Bow before God that you might become nothing and that He might become all.

## Notes

1. David Vaughan, *A Divine Light: The Spiritual Leadership of Jonathan Edwards* (Nashville: Cumberland House, 2007), 153.
2. George M. Marsden, *Jonathan Edwards: A Life* (New Haven, Conn./London: Yale University Press, 2003), 45.
3. Iain Murray, *Jonathan Edwards: A New Biography* (Edinburgh: Banner of Truth Trust, 1987), 41.
4. Ibid., 42.
5. Ibid.
6. Marsden, *Jonathan Edwards: A Life*, 45.
7. Ibid.
8. Jonathan Edwards, "Personal Narrative," in *The Works of Jonathan Edwards, Vol. 16, Letters and Personal Writings*, ed. George S. Claghorn (New Haven, Conn.: Yale University Press, 1998), 796.
9. Ibid.
10. Ibid.
11. Edwards, "Diary," *Works* (Yale), *Vol. 16*, 769.
12. Ibid., 761.
13. Ibid., 765.

14. Ibid., 767.

15. Edwards, "Personal Narrative," *Works* (Yale), *Vol. 16*, 803.

16. Ibid., 802.

17. Ibid., 803.

18. Edwards, "Diary," *Works* (Yale), *Vol. 16,* 766.

19. Ibid.

20. Ibid., 777.

21. Ibid., 764.

22. Marsden, *Jonathan Edwards: A Life*, 56.

23. Edwards, "Diary," *Works* (Yale), *Vol. 16,* 776.

24. Ibid., 775.

25. Ibid., 761.

26. Ibid., 778.

27. Edwards, "Personal Narrative," *Works* (Yale), *Vol. 16*, 802.

# CHAPTER SIX

# The Precipice of Eternity

*Edwards spent his whole life preparing to die.*[1]
—GEORGE MARSDEN

The pursuit of God's glory is never a mystical experience disconnected from the nitty-gritty of everyday life. Neither is it an ivory-tower existence divorced from the practical responsibilities of this world. If anyone purposes to bring honor to God, this highest of all pursuits will influence even the most seemingly insignificant areas of his existence.

For Jonathan Edwards, glorifying God included something as basic as the proper use of his time in light of eternity. He knew that if he was to honor God, he must use the time that had been entrusted to him wisely. Each moment was priceless. He could not waste time *and* bring honor to God. In Edwards' view, time was infinitely valuable and utterly irreplaceable when lost. He understood God had sovereignly allotted him a specific measure of time, a precise number of years, days, hours, and even seconds in which he would live. His days, literally, were numbered. He was merely a steward of his time and would be accountable to God for its use.

That is not to say that Edwards was myopically focused on the seconds of his days. He also grasped the crucial importance of seeing the big picture. To that end, he sought to keep his mind riveted upon the sobering realities of his own death, Christ's return, and the world to come in order to help himself live for God in the present.

Concerning Edwards' stewardship of time, Don Whitney writes: "At the root of all discipline is the disciplined use of time. Without this one, there are no other disciplines. . . . Edwards recognized this early on, and thus three of the very first of his famous Resolutions—in this case, numbers 5 to 7—were on the stewardship of time."[2] George Marsden writes, "true to his Puritan heritage, he often came back to the use of time."[3]

In short, Edwards was convinced that he stood upon the precipice of eternity and must invest his time shrewdly with the greatest rate of return. With his life before him, this young Puritan purposed that every moment of his life would strategically count for God's glory. He saw his *life* and his *time* as inseparably connected. Resolutions 5, 7, 11, 19, and 50 deal time, death, and eternity.

## LIMITED TIME

Edwards understood he could lose money and potentially recoup it later. He could lose his health and yet recover it. He could even lose a relationship and later restore it. But time lost could never be regained. Thus, in the fifth resolution, Edwards purposed to put his time to maximum use:

> 5. Resolved, never to lose one moment of time; but improve it the most profitable way I possibly can.

Young Edwards had many demands on his time. When he wrote this resolution, he was serving as an interim pastor and was discovering the many responsibilities that are borne by ministers. He also had work to complete toward his master's degree. In addition, Edwards had many interests, including the natural sciences and world events. He desired to prioritize his activities so as to best glorify God in each moment.

So zealous was Edwards to improve his use of time that he calculated ways to gain minutes from tasks large and small: "Thursday night, Jan. 2. These things established,— That time gained in things of lesser importance, is as much gained in things of greater; that a minute gained in times of confusion, conversation, or in a journey, is as good as a minute gained in my study, at my most retire times; and so, in general, that a minute gained at one time is as good as at another."[4] *Any* time gained was precious to Edwards.

He was especially aware of his responsibility to improve the use of his time in connection with his battle against his sin. In his diary Edwards wrote: "Sabbath day, Jan. 6, at night. Much concerned about the improvement of precious time. Intend to live in continual mortification, without ceasing, and even to weary myself thereby as long as I am in this world, and never to expect or desire any worldly ease or pleasure."[5] Thus, time spent putting sin to death was well-spent.

In the above entry, Edwards stated that he was "much concerned" about the "improvement" of his time. He saw he must always seek the most effective and strategic use of his time according to the will of God. Some demands on his time were matters of "the tyranny of the urgent"—they required his attention but were not priorities. These concerns must be given less time. Other matters, far more important, must be prioritized and given more time. Still other matters required his attention at an hour of the day when he was more alert.

## FINAL HOUR

To help himself value his time, Edwards determined to keep an eye on the final hour of his life—the hour in which he would stand on the threshold of his entrance into the presence of God. In resolution 7, Edwards vowed:

> 7. Resolved, never to do anything, which I should be afraid to do, if it were the last hour of my life.

This resolution was primarily intended to help Edwards in the mortification of his sin. He anticipated that asking himself whether he would engage in a particular activity if he had only one hour to live would help him steer clear of temptation. He was persuaded he would not want to pass into God's presence after committing any sin. If he could say that he ought to avoid any activity in his final hour, he would know that he ought to avoid it at any point in his Christian walk. This perspective would restrain his sinful thoughts, activities, and words.

Edwards often found much sanctifying value in focusing on the certainty of his death. When combating worldly thoughts, he wrote in his diary: "Sabbath morning, Sept. 1. When I am violently beset with worldly thoughts, for a relief, to think of death, and the doleful circumstances of it."[6] Thoughts of death turned his mind to eternal realities, making worldly temptations of the moment seem empty and unattractive. Living as if he was in his *last* hour helped him keep sinful things at a distance.

Thoughts of death also helped Edwards keep a proper perspective on possessions. In his diary, he asked himself a probing question: "Monday, Feb. 3. Let every thing have the value now which it will have upon a sick bed; and frequently, in my pursuits of whatever kind, let this question come into my mind. 'How much shall I value this upon my death-bed?'"[7] Edwards believed that contemplating his deathbed scene forced him to value what was most important in the present.

Contemplating his death even helped Edwards prepare

himself *for* death. Edwards recorded: "Friday morning, July 5. Last night, when thinking what I should wish I had done, that I had not done, if I was then to die; I thought I should wish, that I had been more importunate with God to fit me for death, and lead me into all truth, and that I might not be deceived about the state of my soul."[8] Though Edwards wrote these words as a teenager, in the full bloom of life, he wanted to be prepared to meet his Lord with His approval.

Focusing upon the end of life had the effect of helping Edwards prioritize what was most important in his life. This perspective restrained his sinful thoughts, activities, and words. Further, it helped him choose the highest ends in life. Not all choices in the use of his time were between good and evil. Some of the most difficult choices were between good, better, and best. Always living as if he were at the end of his life caused him to live for what is best, the glory of God.

## IMMEDIATE ACTION

As Edwards became aware of an action he must undertake, he sought to accomplish it *immediately*. In resolution 11, he applied this determination to theological problems:

> 11. Resolved, when I think of any theorem in divinity to be solved, immediately to do what I can towards solving it, if circumstances don't hinder.

As Edwards studied and read, he often came upon "theorems in divinity," or theological issues, that were not easily understood. In such cases, he vowed to address the doctrinal difficulty immediately in order to come to a proper understanding. Time must not be wasted, he reasoned, in solving such weighty matters.

In this resolution, Edwards recognized the sovereignty of God, for he added, "if circumstances don't hinder." Even in solving difficult issues in theology, Edwards humbly submitted himself to the overruling hand of God.

Edwards believed procrastination to be an obstacle to God's glory. Delayed obedience is no obedience. Slowness to carry out a task dishonors Him. Thus, Edwards felt he must do his duties as quickly as possible. But he candidly admitted that he struggled with procrastination. He wrote: "Wednesday, Jan. 9. I do not seem to be half so careful to improve time, to do every thing quick, and in as short a time as I possibly can, nor to be perpetually engaged to think about religion, as I was yesterday and the day before, nor indeed as I have been at certain times, perhaps a twelvemonth ago."[9] On another occasion he noted: "Saturday night, May 11. I have been to blame, the month past, in not laying violence enough to my inclination, to force myself to a better improvement of time."[10] Edwards sensed that he must be always pushing himself with "violence" to improve the use of his time.

## LAST TRUMPET

Edwards believed that not all Christians would leave this world by death. Some would be alive at the time of the second coming of Christ. Reflecting that belief, in an echo of his seventh resolution, Edwards wrote:

> 19. Resolved, never to do anything, which I should be afraid to do, if I expected it would not be above an hour, before I should hear the last trump.

With this resolution, Edwards purposed that he would never do anything that would bring him regret if Christ should return at that moment. Knowing that Christ could burst onto the scene unexpectedly restrained him from certain attitudes and activities.

Although Edwards' eschatology was yet to be developed when he wrote his "Resolutions," he loved biblical prophecies concerning Christ's return. Stephen J. Stein notes: "The book of Revelation fascinated Jonathan Edwards. . . . For him the Apocalypse came alive with each new reading. . . . Edwards spent long hours studying the Revelation, the only book of the Bible he favored with a separate commentary; that preoccupation . . . spanned the full range of his years."[11] John Gerstner writes that the return of Christ was a "controlling concept in Edwards' thinking."[12]

In time, Edwards became convinced that the return of Christ was imminent. Gerstner writes: "Edwards thought that the latter days were rapidly approaching. . . . [Edwards believed] Scripture does not allow the calculation of the exact date of the Parousia, but it does indicate the general period."[13] Edwards himself asserted: "Christ will appear in the glory of His Father, with all His holy angels, coming in the clouds of heaven. . . .This will be a most unexpected sight to the wicked world; it will come as a cry at midnight. . . . But with respect to the saints, it shall be a joyful and most glorious sight to them. . . . Thus to see their Redeemer coming in the clouds of heaven, will fill their hearts full of gladness."[14]

Anticipation of Christ's return compelled Edwards in his pursuit of holiness. He desired that when the last trumpet should sound, he would not be found in sin but in godly living.

## FUTURE WORLD

As Edwards looked beyond this life, he focused on the future world in which he would find himself one day. In resolution 50, Edwards purposed to do his utmost to live in a way he would still regard as best even when he arrived in that world:

> 50. Resolved, I will act so as I think I shall judge would have been best, and most prudent, when I come into the future world. July 5, 1723.

Edwards knew he would have a very different perspective after he was taken to heaven and glorified. No longer would sin cloud his thinking. Finally, he would see clearly how best to live for God's glory. But Edwards wanted that perspective right away, so he set out to try to ascertain how he would think when he arrived there.

Edwards was quite honest about his need to be weaned from this world and become concerned with the next. He wrote:

Wednesday, May 1, forenoon. . . . Lord, grant that from hence I may learn to withdraw thoughts, affections, desires, and expectations entirely from the world, and may fix them upon the heavenly state, where there is fullness of joy; where reigns heavenly, sweet, calm, and delightful love without alloy; where there are continually the dearest expressions of this love; where there is the enjoyment of this love without ever parting; and where those persons, who appear so lovely in this world, will be inexpressibly more lovely, and full of love to us. How sweetly will those, who thus mutually love, join together in singing the praises of God and the Lamb. How full will it fill us with joy, to think that this enjoyment, these sweet exercises, will never cease or come to an end, but will last to all eternity.[15]

Edwards desired to live with his heart riveted upon heaven so that he might better live for God's glory in the present. The glories that awaited him before the throne of God pulled him forward as he lived here.

## LIVING WITHOUT REGRETS

Keeping the weighty realities of time, death, Christ's return, and heaven before him helped Edwards gain an eternal perspective. He lived as if he was always ready to step out of this world into the next. Such a lifestyle, in turn, helped him fulfill yet another of his resolutions. He wrote:

> 52. I frequently hear persons in old age say how they would live, if they were to live their lives over again: resolved, that I will live just so as I can think I shall wish I had done, supposing I live to old age. July 8, 1723.

Edwards passionately desired to live in such a way that he would not be filled with regrets over a wasted life someday. He stated that he often had heard old men confide that they wished they could relive their lives, charting different paths and pursuing different goals. Edwards was determined that it would *not* be so with him.

Of course, avoiding a day of regrets required Edwards to take significant steps early in life. The same steps must be taken by each one of us *now* if we are to meet the future with contentment. Like Edwards, we must make the pursuit of God's glory our highest goal and deepest calling.

Jonathan Edwards lived without regrets. Will *you*?

## Notes

1. George Marsden, *Jonathan Edwards: A Life* (New Haven, Conn./London: Yale University Press, 2003), 490.
2. Donald S. Whitney, "Pursuing a Passion for God through Spiritual Disciplines: Learning from Jonathan Edwards," *A God-Entranced Vision of All Things: The Legacy of Jonathan Edwards,* eds. John Piper and Justin Taylor (Wheaton, Ill.: Crossway, 2004), 123–124.
3. Marsden, *Jonathan Edwards: A Life*, 51.
4. Jonathan Edwards, "Diary," *The Works of Jonathan Edwards, Vol. 16, Letters and Personal Writings*, ed. George S. Claghorn (New Haven, Conn.: Yale University Press, 1998), 783.
5. Ibid., 761.
6. Ibid., 780.
7. Ibid., 784.
8. Ibid., 774.
9. Ibid., 761.
10. Ibid., 769.
11. Stephen J. Stein, "Introduction," *The Works of Jonathan Edwards, Vol. 5, Apocalyptic Writings*, ed. Stephen J. Stein (New Haven, Conn.: Yale University Press, 1977), 1.
12. John H. Gerstner, *The Rational Biblical Theology of Jonathan Edwards, Vol. III* (Powhatan, Va.: Berea Publications, 1993), 484.
13. Ibid.
14. Jonathan Edwards, *The Works of Jonathan Edwards, Vol. 9, A History of the Work of Redemption*, ed. John F. Wilson (New Haven, Conn.: Yale University Press, 1989), 494–495
15. Edwards, "Diary," *Works* (Yale), *Vol. 16*, 768.

# CHAPTER SEVEN

# The Passion of Discipline

*Edwards maintained the rigor of his study schedule only with strict attention to diet and exercise. Everything was calculated to optimize his efficiency and power in study.*[1]

—JOHN PIPER

P ossessing an inner drive that has been described as being of "Pauline proportions,"[2] Jonathan Edwards was relentless in his pursuit of holiness. "His youthful ambition was to be the most 'complete Christian' of his age," George S. Claghorn explains. "He accepted the strenuous effort involved and dedicated every thought, every action, to the promotion of that goal. His sole ambition was to realize his greatest potential and maximum usefulness for the glory of God."[3] In short, Edwards was wholehearted in his passion for God and His kingdom.

By his own testimony, Edwards desired to be "wrapt up to God in heaven and, be as it were swallowed up in Him."[4] Willing to pay any price necessary in this endeavor, Edwards set out "to lose all sense of personal selfhood"[5] in order to pursue Christ. Edwards believed "complacency was a great impediment to the Christian life,"[6] that halfheartedness would never produce holiness, so he refused to allow it in himself. True to his convictions, Edwards "never abandoned his belief in the value of strict spiritual disciplines."[7]

This chapter will focus on Edwards' personal discipline. Refusing to live in an unstructured manner, he purposed to know and serve God through a highly-regimented life. Resolutions 6, 20, 28, and 61 express aspects of this singleminded pursuit.

## WHOLEHEARTED DEVOTION

Edwards' desire for personal discipline began with a fundamental commitment to live life to the fullest. He refused to be content with mere existence, simply going through the motions of meaningless activities. For Edwards, true living necessitated personal discipline in every area of the Christian life. For this reason, Edwards wrote in his sixth resolution that he never would live the Christian life in halfhearted complacency, but always would be pressing forward to greater degrees of godliness. He wrote:

6. Resolved, to live with all my might, while I do live.

This short resolution says much about Edwards. He was willing to commit the entirety of his being to his pursuit of holiness. He would live wholeheartedly for Christ, tolerating no side loyalties or competing allegiances. He would pour all his energies into every endeavor as long as he lived. He would never allow himself to grow slack in his pursuit of God's will, but would entirely engage in all that he undertook for Christ. Edwards purposed that he would *really* live. Wherever he was, he would be *all* there.

In an echo of resolution 63, Edwards pledged in his diary to seek to be the most complete Christian in his generation. He set himself the goal of living at a level of closeness to God and fullness of spirituality that no other Christian was achieving: "Monday, Jan. 14. . . . Supposing there was never but one complete Christian, in all respects of a right stamp, having Christianity shining in its true luster, at a time in the world; resolved to act just as I would do, if I strove with all my might to be that one, that should be in my time."[8]

This is not to suggest that Edwards always lived with all his might. In fact, he recorded some of his struggles to remain consistent in his pursuit. Sometimes he found himself negligent in his spiritual disciplines. If he were more steadfastly committed, he believed, he could do twice as much for the Lord:

Saturday, Feb. 23. I find myself miserably negligent, and that I might do twice the business that I do, if I were set upon it. See how soon my thoughts of this matter, will be differing from what they are now. I have been indulging a horrid laziness a good while, and did not know it. I can do seven times as much in the same time now, as I can at other times, not because my faculties are in better tune; but because of the fire of diligence that I feel burning within me. If I could but always continue so, I should not meet with one quarter of the trouble. I should run the Christian race much better, and should go out of the world a much better man.[9]

Seeing the Christian life as a race, Edwards vowed to press on to the finish. He would not grow complacent, but strive for the prize and run the race to win (1 Cor. 9:24). To that end, he further resolved to discipline his body (v. 27).

## PHYSICAL REGIMENTATION

Physical discipline was a major aspect of Edwards' whole-hearted commitment to God. Edwards believed restraint and balance should mark every area of his physical life, including his diet, his sleep, and his physical exercise. He believed that his body was the temple in which he worshiped and served God. Therefore, his physical life must be disciplined if his spiritual life was to be developed. Edwards pledged himself in resolution 20 to some practical steps toward this end:

> 20. Resolved, to maintain the strictest temperance in eating and drinking.

The word *temperance* means "moderation" or "restraint," and this is what Edwards sought to achieve in his eating and drinking. George Marsden notes that Edwards maintained a "Spartan diet."[10] However, he "was constantly experimenting with himself, seeing how much he needed to eat out of necessity and avoiding all excesses that would dull his mind or rouse his passions. Throughout his life, observers commented on his strict eating habits and often emaciated appearance. Though he lived in the midst of the world, he did so as an ascetic."[11] John Piper adds that Edwards "carefully observed the effects of the different sorts of food, and selected those which best suited his constitution, and rendered him most fit for mental labor."[12]

But Edwards' pursuit of temperance was not without struggle. He noted he could forget his resolve while in the act of eating:

> Saturday night, Feb. 15. I find that when eating, I cannot be convinced in the time of it, that if I should eat more, I should exceed the bounds of strict temperance, though I have had the experience of two years of the

like; and yet, as soon as I have done, in three minutes I am convinced of it. But yet, when I eat again, and remember it, still, while eating, I am fully convinced that I have not eaten what is but for nature, nor can I be convinced that my appetite and feeling is as it was before. It seems to me that I shall be somewhat faint if I leave off then; but when I have finished, I am convinced again, and so it is from time to time.[13]

Edwards also noted that he needed to exercise special care to restrain himself when a meal was especially pleasing to his tastes or offered a variety of dishes: "Sabbath day, Feb. 23. . . . When I am at a feast or a meal, that very well pleases my appetite, I must not merely take care to leave off with as much of an appetite as at ordinary meals; for when there is a great variety of dishes, I may do that, after I have eaten twice as much as at other meals, is sufficient."[14]

On another occasion, he admitted he was guilty of neglecting to maintain his strict oversight in matters of food, drink, and sleep while on a trip: "Saturday morning, June 15, at Windsor. Have been to blame, this journey, with respect to strict temperance, in eating, drinking and sleeping, and in suffering too small matters to give interruption to my wonted chain of religious exercise."[15]

The value of carefully limiting his diet was clear to Edwards. In his diary, he articulated a number of benefits: "Tuesday, Sept. 2. By a sparingness in diet, and eating, as much as may be, what is light and easy of digestion, I shall doubtless be able to think clearer, and shall gain time. 1st, by lengthening out my life. 2dly, shall need less time for digestion after meals. 3rdly, shall be able to study closer without wrong to my health. 4thly, shall need less time to sleep. 5thly, shall seldomer be troubled with the headache."[16]

Beyond that, Edwards saw a direct connection between his physical habits—eating, drinking, and sleeping—and his spiritual sharpness. Self-control in his physical life, he realized, affected self-control in his spiritual life. Both areas required self-denial. Edwards wrote: "Thursday, Jan. 10, about noon. . . . I think I find myself much more sprightly and healthy, both in body and mind, for my self-denial in eating, drinking, and sleeping."[17]

Edwards' limits on his food intake became borderline detrimental at times. Edwards noted that his discipline in eating was so strict, it often caused him to become physically weak. To this point, Edwards wrote: "Saturday, Jan. 12, in the morning. . . . It is suggested to me, that too constant a mortification, and too vigorous application to religion, may be prejudicial to health. But nevertheless, I will plainly feel it and experience it, before I cease, on this account. It is no matter how much tired and weary I am, if my health is not impaired."[18]

Edwards also carefully regulated his sleep patterns. Because of the importance to him of time alone with God, Edwards adopted the practice of rising in the pre-dawn hours. He believed Christ exemplified this pattern both in His life (Mark 1:35) and His resurrection: "January 1728. I think Christ has recommended rising early in the morning, by His rising from the grave very early."[19] Marsden writes: "Edwards usually rose at four or five in the morning in order to spend thirteen hours in his study. . . . The discipline was part of a constant, heroic effort to make his life a type of Christ."[20] Edwards was always eager to begin his daily work.

Finally, physical exercise was important to Edwards. He felt his body must be active if his mind was to remain alert, so he permitted himself to engage in activities such as chopping wood, horseback riding, and the like. Piper writes: "In addition to watching his diet so as to maximize his mental powers, he also took heed to his need for exercise. In the winter he would chop firewood a half-hour each day, and in the summer he would ride into the fields and walk alone in meditation."[21] Ultimately, Edwards believed that exercise helped keep his heart strong toward God.

## SPIRITUAL DISCIPLINES

Edwards also strictly regimented himself in the spiritual disciplines of the Christian life, such as Bible study, theological reading, meditation, prayer, and singing. Such spiritual disciplines are necessary for spiritual health; as Donald Whitney writes, they promote "intimacy with Christ and conformity (both internal and external) to Christ."[22] For this reason, Edwards gave himself to spiritual disciples with great diligence. We see a clear manifestation of this disciple in resolution 28:

28. Resolved, to study the Scriptures so steadily, constantly and frequently, as that I may find, and plainly perceive myself to grow in the knowledge of the same.

Edwards certainly pursued time in the Word with great diligence. "Scripture was central to his conversion," Michael Haykin notes. "Not surprisingly, he would . . . maintain that Scripture needs to be central in all . . . Christian piety."[23] The devotion with which Edwards undertook Bible reading and study yielded, Haykin writes, a "profound Bible knowledge" and an "uncommon acquaintance with the Bible."[24] Samuel Hopkins, Edwards' brother-in-law and his biographer, wrote that "he studied the Bible more than all other books, and more than most other divines do."[25] This "Word-shaped spirituality"[26] would govern his entire life.

Edwards wrote of the strength he found in the Scriptures: "Saturday, May 23. How it comes about I know not; but I have remarked it hitherto, that at those times when I have read the Scripture most, I have evermore been most lively, and in the best frames."[27] On another occasion, he added: "Tuesday morning, Aug. 13. . . . I find it would be very much to advantage, to be thoroughly acquainted with the Scriptures."[28] He believed experientially that the Scriptures were "life-giving": "I have sometimes had an affecting sense of the excellency of the word of God, as a word of life; as the light of life; a sweet, excellent, life-giving word: accompanied with a thirsting after that word, that it might dwell richly in my heart."[29]

Edwards' disciplined approach to Scripture was by no means drudgery for him. To the contrary, Bible intake delighted him because it yielded the knowledge of God:

> I had then, and at other times, the greatest delight in the holy Scriptures, of any book whatsoever. Oftentimes in reading it, every word seemed to touch my heart. I felt an harmony between something in my heart, and those sweet and powerful words. I seemed often to see so much light, exhibited by every sentence, and such a refreshing ravishing food communicated, that I could not get along in reading. Used oftentimes to dwell long on one sentence, to see the wonders contained in it; and yet almost every sentence seemed to be full of wonders.[30]

Edwards also made time to read various theological and polemical books. For Edwards, Bible study required serious digging into the text, and these other works aided his understanding. Edwards wrote: "Tuesday morning, Aug. 13. . . . When I am reading doctrinal books or books of controversy, I can proceed with abundantly more confidence; can see upon what footing and foundation I stand."[31]

Nevertheless, Edwards did not let himself be seduced into spending excessive time in books written by men to the neglect to the Word of God. It was far better, he wrote, to spend additional time studying or reflecting on the Scriptures than to read books that were "not very good." In his diary, he pledged: "Wednesday night, Aug. 28. When I want books to read; yea, when I have not very good books, not to spend time in reading them, but in reading the Scriptures, in perusing Resolutions, Reflections, etc., in writing on types of the Scripture, and other things, in studying the languages, and in spending more time in private duties."[32]

Further, Edwards set aside time for quiet meditation on Scripture, contemplating the glories of Christ in His Word. Hopkins noted that Edwards spent much time "in devout reading of God's word and meditation upon it."[33] The spiritual discipline of meditation on Scripture "was part of Edwards' Puritan heritage . . . [and] central to Edwards' walk with God."[34] Whitney writes: "Meditation on Scripture was Edwards's practice from his first days as a disciple of Jesus. . . . Edwards seemed particularly fond of meditating on Scripture while walking in solitude or while on horseback, whether riding for relaxation or on a journey."[35] This involved thinking in "a prolonged and focused way about a truth in a biblical text."[36]

Such meditation in solitude proved to be a crucial part of his spiritual life, producing great joy in his heart. Haykin writes that an inward satisfaction "gripped his soul as he meditated upon what Scripture says about God and Christ and Their utterly free and sovereign grace in salvation."[37] Reflecting upon the months immediately after his conversion, Edwards recalled: "I very frequently used to retire into a solitary place, on the banks of Hudson's River, at some distance from the city, for contemplation on divine things, and secret converse with God; and had many sweet hours there."[38]

Sometimes Edwards found his meditations so satisfying that he even would skip a meal: "Jan. 22, 1734. I judge that it is best, when I am in a good frame for divine contemplation, or engaged in reading the Scriptures, or any study of divine subjects, that ordinarily, I will not be interrupted by going to dinner, but will forego my dinner, rather than be broke off."[39] Such was Edwards' love for communion with God.

Edwards also believed that prayer was an essential spiritual discipline. As Whitney notes, "the idea of a Christian who did not pray was preposterous. It was inconceivable that anyone could know the God he knew and not be compelled by the sweetness, love, and satisfaction found in God to pray. It seemed contrary to Edwards' understanding of Scripture that anyone could be indwelled by the Spirit who causes God's children to 'cry out, "Abba! Father!"' (Rom. 8:15; cf. Gal. 4:6) and yet not cry out to the Father in regular private prayer."[40]

Edwards set himself to come to God in prayer at regular intervals throughout the day. "Edwards was so devoted to prayer," Whitney writes, "that it is hard to find a daily routine for him that wasn't permeated with it. He prayed alone when he arose. . . . He prayed over his studies, and he prayed as he walked in the evenings. Prayer was both a discipline and a part of his leisure."[41]

However, Edwards confided to his diary that he often struggled to maintain regular prayer: "Monday morning, May 6. I think it best commonly to come before God three times in a day, except I find a great inaptitude to that duty."[42] On another occasion, Edwards expressed the same struggle to maintain his times of prayer while on a journey: "Sabbath-day morning, May 19. With respect to my journey last week, I was not careful enough, to watch opportunities of solemnly approaching to God, three times a day. The last week, when I was about to take up the Wednesday Resolution,[43] it was proposed to me, in my thoughts, to omit it until I got home again, because there would be a more convenient opportunity."[44]

Finally, Edwards often worshiped God privately by lifting up his voice in the singing of psalms. The Word of God produced within him the worship of God. Whitney notes: "Edwards could not conceive of private worship without [singing]. . . . Edwards spoke of his private, spontaneous songs to God as that which 'seemed natural' and flowed from the sweetness of his contemplations of God."[45] Thus, Edwards pledged: "Sabbath evening, Sept. 22. To praise God, by singing psalms in prose, and by singing forth the meditations of my heart in prose."[46]

These diverse disciplines—Bible study, theological reading, meditation, prayer, and singing—worked hand in hand, the one supporting the other, in Edwards' pursuit of holiness. These religious duties helped Edwards maintain a vibrant communion with God. His theology led to doxology.

## STEADFAST FERVOR

Edwards was often disappointed in his shortcomings in his pursuit of God's glory. In his diary, he frequently confessed to being "dull," "dry," and "listless" in his spiritual fervency. Consequently, in resolution 61, Edwards purposed that he would not give in to spiritual apathy:

> 61. Resolved, that I will not give way to that list-lessness which I find unbends and relaxes my mind from being fully and fixedly set on religion, whatever excuse I may have for it—that what my listlessness inclines me to do, is best to be done, etc. May 21 and July 13, 1723.

For Edwards, "listlessness" was a state in which his mind was less than fully fixed on spiritual things. To become list-less was to lose his spiritual edge, to become lukewarm and lackadaisical, and for Edwards, there was no excuse for it. This resolution was so important to him that he dated it twice, an indication it was doubly affirmed to his heart.

Despite such remarkable resolve, Edwards experienced seasons of drought. Some of his diary entries reveal these times in his life:

Dec. 21, Friday. This day, and yesterday, I was exceedingly dull, dry and dead.[47]

Saturday, Dec. 29. About sunset this day, dull and lifeless.[48]

Tuesday, Jan. 1. Have been dull for several days. Examined whether I have not been guilty of negligence today; and resolved, No.[49]

However, Edwards also recorded that the Holy Spirit often revived his spiritual desires. When beholding the glories of Christ, he believed the Spirit enlightened his heart with the beauty of God's holiness: "Saturday, Dec. 22, 1722. This day revived by God's Spirit. Affected with the sense of the excellency of holiness. Felt more exercise of love to Christ than usual. Have also felt sensible repentance of sin, because it was committed against so merciful and good a God. This night made the 37th Resolution."[50]

But while depending on the Spirit for revival, Edwards was committed to doing all he could to remain fervent in his love for God and Christ. Two days later, Edwards wrote: "Monday, Dec. 24. Higher thoughts than usual of the excellency of Jesus Christ and His kingdom."[51] This rejuvenation was the result of Edwards declaring his ways to God and laying open his soul to Him, as well as his reading of the sermons of the noted Puritan Thomas Manton on Psalm 119.

## A DISCIPLINED PURSUIT OF HOLINESS

Edwards' tenacious sense of mission brought all areas of his life under disciplined control. No aspect of his life went unscrutinized—eating, drinking, sleeping, exercise, Scripture study, theological reading, meditation, prayer, worship, and his affections. In all of this, Edwards made careful and regular inquiry regarding his progress and necessary alterations.

Through self-discipline, Edwards sought to make the pursuit of the glory of God concrete and specific in his life. Is it any wonder, given such strict self-control, that God used Edwards so greatly?

Edwards stands as a positive example for all believers today. He shows us how a Christian may discipline himself for the purpose of godliness. May the Lord give grace to all who seek to live with the strict commitment of a champion athlete, striving to receive the prize on the last day. May we all run in such a way as to win.

### Notes

1. John Piper, *God's Passion for His Glory: Living the Vision of Jonathan Edwards* (Wheaton, Ill.: Crossway, 1998), 56.
2. George S. Claghorn, "Introduction," *The Works of Jonathan Edwards, Vol. 16, Letters and Personal Writings*, ed. George S. Claghorn (New Haven, Conn.: Yale University Press, 1998), 741.
3. Ibid.
4. Jonathan Edwards, "Personal Narrative," *Works* (Yale), *Vol. 16*, 792.

5. Philip F. Gura, *Jonathan Edwards: America's Evangelical* (New York: Hill and Wang, 2005), 33.

6. Ibid., 35.

7. George Marsden, *Jonathan Edwards: A Life* (New Haven, Conn./London: Yale University Press, 2003), 53.

8. Edwards, "Diary," *Works* (Yale), *Vol. 16*, 764.

9. Ibid., 767.

10. Marsden, *Jonathan Edwards: A Life*, 251.

11. Ibid., 51.

12. Piper, *God's Passion for His Glory: Living the Vision of Jonathan Edwards*, 56.

13. Edwards, "Diary," *Works* (Yale), *Vol. 16*, 784–785.

14. Ibid., 785.

15. Ibid., 772.

16. Ibid., 786.

17. Ibid., 761.

18. Ibid., 763.

19. Ibid., 789.

20. Marsden, *Jonathan Edwards: A Life*, 133.

21. Piper, *God's Passion for His Glory: Living the Vision of Jonathan Edwards*, 56.

22. Donald S. Whitney, "Pursuing a Passion for God through Spiritual Disciplines: Learning from Jonathan Edwards," in *A God-Entranced Vision of All Things: The Legacy of Jonathan Edwards*, eds. John Piper and Justin Taylor (Wheaton, Ill.: Crossway, 2004), 110.

23. Michael A. G. Haykin, *"A Sweet Flame": Piety in the Letters of Jonathan Edwards* (Grand Rapids: Reformation Heritage Books, 2007), 5.

24. Ibid., 7.

25. Samuel Hopkins, "The Life and Character of the Late Reverend Mr. Jonathan Edwards," in *Jonathan Edwards: A Profile*, ed. David Levin (New York: Hill and Wang, 1969), 40–41.

26. Haykin, *"A Sweet Flame": Piety in the Letters of Jonathan Edwards*, 4.

27. Edwards, "Diary," *Works* (Yale), *Vol. 16*, 785–786.

28. Ibid., 779.

29. Ibid., 801.

30. Ibid., 797.

31. Ibid., 779.

32. Ibid., 780.

33. Hopkins, "The Life and Character of the Late Reverend Mr. Jonathan Edwards," in *Jonathan Edwards: A Profile*, 39.

34. Haykin, *"A Sweet Flame": Piety in the Letters of Jonathan Edwards*, 6.
35. Whitney, "Pursuing a Passion for God through Spiritual Disciplines: Learning from Jonathan Edwards," in *A God-Entranced Vision of All Things: The Legacy of Jonathan Edwards*, 113.
36. Ibid.
37. Haykin, *"A Sweet Flame": Piety in the Letters of Jonathan Edwards*, 6.
38. Edwards, "Diary," *Works* (Yale), *Vol. 16*, 797.
39. Ibid., 789.
40. Whitney, "Pursuing a Passion for God through Spiritual Disciplines: Learning from Jonathan Edwards," in *A God-Entranced Vision of All Things: The Legacy of Jonathan Edwards*, 115.
41. Ibid., 114.
42. Edwards, "Diary," *Works* (Yale), *Vol. 16*, 769.
43. "The Wednesday Resolution" was Edwards' nickname for resolution 16. See chapter 8.
44. Ibid., 770–771.
45. Whitney, "Pursuing a Passion for God through Spiritual Disciplines: Learning from Jonathan Edwards," in *A God-Entranced Vision of All Things: The Legacy of Jonathan Edwards*, 115–116.
46. Edwards, "Diary," *Works* (Yale), *Vol. 16*, 781.
47. Ibid., 759.
48. Ibid., 760.
49. Ibid.
50. Ibid., 759.
51. Ibid., 760.

# CHAPTER EIGHT

# The Practice of Love

*The value of Edwards's work is not found merely in his lucid and penetrating mind. What is most singular is his combination of rational analysis with spiritual ardor. Here was a man whose heart was aflame with love and devotion for the sweetness and excellence of Christ. His work exudes authentic religious affection. He was, above all things, a lover of God. . . . The things of God captured Edwards's heart and invested it with an all-consuming passion of love.*[1]

—R. C. SPROUL

onathan Edwards believed that as surely as night follows day and summer follows spring, his Christian duty to love others flowed out of his fervent love for God. These affections—love for God *and* for others—are bound together. The more one's devotion to God deepens, the more he will

123

pursue the scriptural commands to abound in love toward his fellow men. Edwards realized that, in Christ, he owed a debt of love that he *must* repay. He accepted Scripture's teaching that even if he spoke the languages of men and angels, possessed all knowledge, and gave away all that he had, he still would be nothing if he did not display love (1 Cor. 13:1–3). The love he showed toward others would demonstrate his love for God.

Thus, the practice of love was vitally important to Edwards—as it should be for every Christian. As a result, when this young Puritan pastor took pen in hand to record his "Resolutions," he pledged to love others—whether they be friend or foe—in whatever expression necessary. For Edwards, love was an essential part of the pursuit of holiness.

Edwards is often stereotyped today as an unhappy individual, cold, clinical, unsmiling, and unloving. This impression has proliferated because, almost twenty years after he wrote his "Resolutions," Edwards delivered a thunderbolt sermon on the final judgment and hell, titled "Sinners in the Hands of an Angry God." This now-famous "fire-and-brimstone" message left his listeners clinging to the edges of their pews in terror. Since then, many have assumed that such an intense preacher could not possibly have been a loving person. What is more, Edwards was "naturally shy and antisocial,"[2] one who preferred serious study over small talk. J. I. Packer writes that he was "grave, taciturn with strangers, and always somewhat withdrawn,"[3] and Elizabeth Dodds describes him as "socially bumbling, barricaded behind the stateliness of the very shy."[4]

This reclusive streak in Edwards has enhanced his misperception as austere, uncaring, and unkind.

But nothing could be further from the truth. Edwards actually possessed a heart full of compassion and mercy toward others. Granted, he was singularly focused on study and remained socially awkward, but as we have seen, he had a passionate love for God that overflowed in a warm affection for people. His love for his wife, Sarah, for example, is unquestioned, as is his devotion to his children. His compassion for others was equally authentic.

As Edwards penned his seventy resolutions, his sincere desire to love others became a recurring theme. We see aspects of this goal in resolutions 13, 14, 16, 33, and 47.

## CHARITABLE ACTS

As Edwards pursued personal holiness, he was persuaded that he must initiate love toward those around him. He could not sit back and wait for others to show love to him first. Therefore, he wrote in resolution 13:

13. Resolved, to be endeavoring to find out fit objects of charity and liberality.

In this pledge, Edwards set himself to "endeavor" to demonstrate love. This is a strong word indicating his resolve to be deliberate and purposeful. He was determined to be self-starting in showing affection toward others. In other words, he would not wait for others to love him; he would show love first.

One significant way in which he carried out this resolution was by trying to initiate conversations about spiritual things. He cared very much about people's eternal destinies and wanted to speak to them about the gospel. He wrote in his "Personal Narrative": "I remember, about that time, I used greatly to long for the conversion of some that I was concerned with. It seemed to me, I could gladly honor them, and with delight be a servant to them, and lie at their feet, if they were but truly holy."[5] He believed he must be careful to capture opportunities to talk to others about God. This is *true* love.

Given how introverted Edwards was, beginning conversations was a challenging task, one at which he knew he needed to improve. He wrote: "Tuesday night, Aug. 20. Not careful enough in watching opportunities of bringing in Christian discourse with a good grace. Do not exercise myself half enough in this holy art; neither have I courage enough to carry it on with a good grace. Vid. September 2."[6] He knew he must take advantage of such divine appointments.

Edwards felt that writing letters was another practical way for him to express Christian love, one which he must practice more often. Noting that he wished to fulfill his social duties, Edwards confessed his shortcomings in this area in his diary: "Nov. 16. . . . One thing wherein I have erred, as I would be complete in all social duties, is, in neglecting to write letters to friends."[7]

From these examples, it may be concluded that Edwards committed himself in this thirteenth resolution to be sensitive to people around him and to show them Christian love in tangible ways. This commitment was further articulated as Edwards penned additional resolutions.

## PATIENT ATTITUDE

For Edwards, an important aspect of exercising Christian love was restraining his temper toward those who irritated or angered him. He understood that the difficulty for the Christian is not in loving people who are easy to love—Jesus said anyone, even an unconverted person, can love his friends (Matt. 5:46). Rather, the challenge lies in loving those with whom it is hard to agree. Christian love requires godly attitudes and actions even toward those who provoke impatience or anger. Edwards composed resolution 14 to help himself react in godly ways:

14. Resolved, never to do anything out of revenge.

From this resolution, it can be assumed that Edwards could be easily provoked and was sometimes tempted to seek retribution. Kenneth P. Minkema notes that the temptation to take revenge was "something with which Edwards apparently struggled."[8]

Edwards admitted that, as a youth, he could be argumentative, especially when he was convinced he was right. The desire to prove his point could escalate into a heated discussion that would damage his relationships with his schoolmates. In his diary, Edwards wrote: "August 28 and January 15. At night. There is much folly, when I am quite sure I am in the right, and others are positive in contradicting me, to enter into a vehement or long debate upon it."[9]

Further evidence of Edwards' struggles with relationships emerges from his time at Yale. Marsden writes that Edwards' intellectual brilliance "did not translate into being liked by his peers."[10] For example, he had a terrible falling out with his college roommate and cousin, Elisha Mix. Their opposite personalities often clashed, Elisha being lighthearted and playful, and Jonathan being serious-minded. These conflicting temperaments caused a great strain in their relationship, as Jonathan could barely endure his younger roommate's immature antics.[11] In another incident, Jonathan befriended an older student, Isaac Stiles, but was too quick to give him personal advice, injuring the bond.[12] Edwards was also overly willing to express "adult-like opinions"[13] about other students' escapades, which infuriated them.

The result of all this conflict was that young Edwards became alienated from his fellow students. Consequently, he struggled to respond toward them with appropriate gentleness and may well have been tempted to retaliate against them in various ways.

In his diary, Edwards recorded several examples of his struggles to resist the temptation to take revenge. One such entry, dated Aug. 24, 1723, concerns an occasion when he secretly hoped for the harm of another:

> Saturday morning, Aug. 24. Have not practiced quite right about revenge; though I have not done anything directly out of revenge, yet, I have perhaps, omitted some things, that I should otherwise have done; or have altered the circumstances and manner of my actions, hoping for a secret sort of revenge thereby. I have felt a little sort of satisfaction, when I thought that such an evil would happen to them by my actions, as would make them repent what they have done. To be satisfied for their repenting, when they repent from a sense of their error, is right. But a satisfaction in their repentance, because of the evil that is brought upon them, is revenge.[14]

On another occasion, troublesome people in the church challenged Edwards' patience, but he knew he needed to show greater forbearance. He wrote in his diary: "Thursday night, July 11. This day, too impatient, at the church meeting. Snares and briars have been in my way, this afternoon. It is good, at such times, for one to manifest good nature, even to one's disadvantage, and so as would be imprudent, at other times."[15]

One virtue that Edwards knew he sorely lacked was gentleness. By his own admission, he could be abrupt in his interpersonal dealings. He felt that a greater degree of gentleness would make his entire character more appealing. Edwards wrote: "Tuesday, Feb. 16. A virtue, which I need in a higher degree, to give a beauty and luster to my behavior, is gentleness. If I had more of an air of gentleness, I should be much mended."[16]

Edwards realized that he must control his reactions toward annoying people in his life. He was determined not to allow his impatience to pull down his emotional state. When others exasperated him, even when he believed he was in the right, Edwards resolved to avoid any trace of personal revenge—but he knew he could not do it alone. Thus, he poured out his heart in a prayer recorded in his diary: "Saturday night, May 4. . . . O that God would help me to discern all the flaws and defects of my temper and conversation, and help me in the difficult work of amending them."[17] Only by God's grace could he restrain himself.

## GRACIOUS WORDS

In his efforts to demonstrate love, Edwards knew he must limit his words in troublesome situations. Few things can be more hurtful than intemperate words spoken in a heated moment. Resolution 16 addressed this potential problem:

> 16. Resolved, never to speak evil of anyone, so that it shall tend to his dishonor, more or less, upon no account except for some real good.

This resolution was so important to Edwards that he referred to it in his diary as "the Wednesday Resolution."[18] The fact that he gave this resolution a nickname makes it clear that speaking evil of others was a sin against which Edwards struggled. This resolution was part of his effort to restrain himself from speaking words that would dishonor others.

At one point, Edwards devised a "stratagem" to help himself conquer this temptation:

Saturday night, May 18. . . . The last Wednesday took up a resolution, to refrain from all manner of evil speaking, for one week, to try it, and see the effect of it: hoping, if that evil speaking, which I used to allow myself in, and to account lawful, agreeably to the resolutions I have formed concerning it, were not lawful, or best, I should hereby discover it, and get the advantage of temptations to it, and so deceive myself, into a strict adherence to my duty, respecting that matter; that corruption, which I cannot conquer by main strength, I may get the victory of by stratagem.[19]

In this diary entry, Edwards expressed the hope that by avoiding "all manner of evil speaking" for a week's time, he might develop a deeper sensitivity to the hurtful words he had been allowing himself to voice. In this we see his efforts to constantly mortify his sin. Having failed to overcome "that corruption" by "main strength," he sought this way to achieve victory over his tongue.

On another occasion, Edwards determined that whenever he was the victim of another person's "faults," he would wait some time before addressing that person: "Saturday, May 22. When I reprove for faults, whereby I am in any way injured, to defer, till the thing is quite over and done with; for that is the way, both to reprove aright, and without the least mixture of spirit, or passion, and to have reproofs effectual, and not suspected."[20] He wanted to point out the other person's wrongdoing after his emotions regarding his own hurt had subsided, lest he say something harmful in the heat of the moment.

## PEACEMAKING SPIRIT

Another vital way in which Edwards sought to show love was by being a peacemaker. In resolution 33, Edwards resolved to pursue peace whenever it could be done without creating harmful effects. He wrote:

> 33. Resolved, always to do what I can towards making, maintaining and establishing peace, when it can be without over-balancing detriment in other respects. Dec. 26, 1722.

He wanted to be a Christian who caused no needless division, but instead helped reconcile people to one another.

However, he recognized in this resolution that peace could not properly be achieved through "over-balancing"—that is, by sacrificing principle. Such peace is *no* peace, only a momentary truce at the price of the truth. For example, Edwards would have preferred to avoid the controversies that later marked his ministries in Northampton and Stockbridge, but in his view, there were biblical principles at stake that he could not sacrifice for the sake of peace.

Still, Edwards took a number of practical steps to become a better peacemaker. One of these was praying for grace that he would be more forgiving toward his enemies. He wrote in his diary: "Saturday night, Apr. 14. I could pray more heartily this night for the forgiveness of my enemies, than ever before. I am somewhat apt, after having asked one petition over many times, to be weary of it; but I am now resolved not to give way to such a disposition."[21]

In this entry, Edwards acknowledged his tendency to grow weary of praying a particular petition many times, and we may conclude that since this admission appears in the context of praying for a forgiving spirit, that Edwards struggled to forgive others. However, it is clear that he *had* persisted in seeking help to forgive, and he rejoiced here that at last he had been able to pray "heartily" that he might pardon his enemies. This persistence in seeking a forgiving spirit reflected his desire to promote peace, not division.

On another occasion, Edwards set himself to refuse to listen to gossip about others. He wrote: "Wednesday [afternoon], July

31. . . . . Never in the least to seek to hear sarcastical relations of others' faults. Never to give credit to anything said against others, except there is very plain reason for it; nor to behave in any respect the otherwise for it."[22] Edwards was determined that when slanderous talk was thrust upon him, he would refuse to believe it without "plain reason" to do so. By guarding himself from receiving potentially untrue accounts of others' actions or words, he helped maintain peace between himself and others.

In an effort to set a good example for his flock, Edwards tried to identify faults in his character so that he would not unknowingly influence others with them. In his diary, he vowed: "Sabbath day, Nov. 22. Considering that bystanders always [copy] some faults which we do not see ourselves, or at least are not so fully sensible of; there are many secret workings of corruption which escape our sight, and others only are sensible of: resolved therefore, that I will, if I can by any convenient means, learn what faults others find in me, or what things they see in me, that appear any way blameworthy, unlovely or unbecoming."[23] Edwards admitted that he could see the sins of others much more readily than he could discover his own iniquities, so he purposed to try to get others' perspectives on his own moral failings.

## COMPASSIONATE HEART

Finally, Edwards felt compelled to pursue whatever was marked by kindness toward others. He decided that his character must be marked by gracious compassion, free from all that was harsh or insensitive. Consequently, he wrote the highly detailed forty-seventh resolution:

> 47. Resolved, to endeavor to my utmost to deny whatever is not most agreeable to a good, and universally sweet and benevolent, quiet, peaceable, contented, easy, compassionate, generous, humble, meek, modest, submissive, obliging, diligent and industrious, charitable, even, patient, moderate, forgiving, sincere temper; and to do at all times what such a temper would lead me to. Examine strictly every week, whether I have done so. Sabbath morning, May 5, 1723.

This resolution was essentially a vow to demonstrate love in ways that were marked by sweetness. The many words for love in this statement reveal the depth of godliness Edwards sought to realize in his life. He pledged to be "benevolent," or full of tender compassion and mercy. Also, he purposed to cultivate a temper that was "quiet," not boisterous or overbearing; "peaceable," or gentle; "easy," meaning easy to get along with; and "generous," marked by open-handed liberality, not clinched-fist stinginess. Further, he wanted to be "humble," lowering himself before others; "meek," or of a lowly spirit; "modest," not seeking to draw attention to himself; "submissive," yielding to others; and "obliging," sensing his duty of love to others. How Edwards interfaced with others was vitally important to God and, thus, to him.

The same aspirations appear in his diary, where he pledged: "Tuesday, Feb. 18. Resolved, to act with sweetness and benevolence, and according to the 47th Resolution, in all bodily dispositions, sick or well, at ease or in pain, sleepy or watchful, and not to suffer discomposure of body to discompose my mind."[24] Here Edwards affirmed that he wanted to display a Christlike temper, especially in times of personal discomfort.

Edwards realized he must show greater sensitivity toward others. One key aspect of that, he felt, was refusing to laugh at the shortcomings of others. Such levity would not display selfless love: He wrote: "Monday morning, Apr. 1. I think it best not to allow myself to laugh at the faults, follies and infirmities of others."[25] Likewise, Edwards set himself to make all his words full of benevolence. He desired that his conversation be marked by kindness, compassion, sympathy, gentleness, thoughtfulness, and consideration: "Saturday noon, Aug. 17. Let there, in the general, be something of benevolence in all that I speak."[26] The picture that emerges here is of a man striving to show forth the love of God in the most minute ways.

## RESOLVED TO LOVE

Edwards knew he must be resolved to love others. Love is not a mere warm, sentimental feeling. Neither is it a shallow, momentary emotion. Instead, love—*true, biblical* love—runs much deeper. It involves an intentional choice of the will to extend the love of God to others. Love, in reality, is a vital part of the pursuit of personal holiness. There can be no growth in godliness without the practice of love. Thus, Edwards elevated the importance of showing love to others around him. Such love, he believed, must be shown in very practical and positive ways, as reflected in these resolutions—in initiating conversations about spiritual things, withholding revenge, restraining anger, showing kindness, and exhibiting grace toward others.

Here is where Christianity must become real for all believers. It is one thing to love God, who is perfectly holy and absolutely righteous. But it is something else entirely to love others, who are far less than perfect. It is even more challenging to love one's enemies. This is the great test of the Christian life—loving the unlovable. But such is the love of God, which we are called to emulate.

The love that God requires of all believers must be purposeful, as Edwards demonstrated. But even if such loving resolve is not written onto paper in the form of a personal resolution, every Christian must choose, deep within, to abound in love toward others. If one is to glorify God, such holy love is absolutely necessary.

May God incline your heart to reach out to love others around you. May you resolve to do so as you pursue personal holiness for the glory of God.

## Notes

1. R. C. Sproul, "Foreword," *Altogether Lovely: Jonathan Edwards on the Glory and Excellency of Jesus Christ* (Morgan, Pa: Soli Deo Gloria, 1997), v.

2. George M. Marsden, *Jonathan Edwards: A Life* (New Haven, Conn./London: Yale University Press, 2003), 37.

3. J. I. Packer, "The Glory of God and the Reviving of Religion," *A God-Entranced Vision of All Things: The Legacy of Jonathan Edwards*, eds. John Piper and Justin Taylor (Wheaton, Ill.: Crossway, 2004), 82.

4. Elisabeth Dodds, *Marriage to a Difficult Man: The Uncommon Union of Jonathan and Sarah Edwards* (Philadelphia, Pa.: Westminster Press, 1971), 11.

5. Jonathan Edwards, "Personal Narrative," in *The Works of Jonathan Edwards, Vol. 16, Letters and Personal Writings*, ed. George S. Claghorn (New Haven, Conn.: Yale University Press, 1998), 799.

6. Edwards, "Diary," *Works* (Yale), *Vol. 16*, 779.

7. Ibid., 788.

8. Kenneth P. Minkema, "Personal Writings," *The Cambridge Companion to Jonathan Edwards* (Cambridge: Cambridge University Press, 2007), 42.

9. Edwards, "Diary," *Works* (Yale), *Vol. 16*, 780–781.

10. Marsden, *Jonathan Edwards: A Life*, 36–37.

11. Ibid., 37.

12. Ibid., 38.

13. Ibid.

14. Edwards, "Diary," *Works* (Yale), *Vol. 16*, 779–780.

15. Ibid., 774.

16. Ibid., 787.

17. Ibid., 769.

18. Minkema, "Personal Writings," *The Cambridge Companion to Jonathan Edwards*, 42.

19. Edwards, "Diary," *Works* (Yale), *Vol. 16*, 770.

20. Ibid., 787.

21. Ibid., 768.

22. Ibid., 777.

23. Ibid., 787. The word *copy*, which appears in brackets in this quote, is in place of *espy*, which is used in the Yale edition. *Copy* appears in the Banner of Truth edition of *The Works* (Edinburgh: Banner of Truth Trust, 1834, 1979), xxxv.

24. Ibid., 785.

25. Ibid., 768.

26. Ibid., 779.

# CHAPTER NINE

# The Posture of Self-Examination

*No man is more relevant to the present condition of Christianity than Jonathan Edwards. None is more needed.*[1]

—D. MARTYN LLOYD-JONES

J onathan Edwards knew that the ongoing assessment of his spiritual life was absolutely necessary in his pursuit of holiness. An unexamined life, in his view, was simply not worth living, for such a life could not bring glory to God. Therefore, he committed himself to the constant surveillance of his Christian walk, regularly auditing his attitudes and appraising his actions.

Years later, in his Northampton pastorate, Edwards urged careful soul-searching from the members of his congregation as they came to the Lord's Supper. He first preached on self-examination in Communion soon after he became the pastor, on March 21, 1731, using 1 Corinthians 11:28 as his text: "Let a person examine himself, then, and so eat of that bread and drink of that cup." In this sermon, Mark Valeri writes, Edwards "focuses on the individual's responsibility to undergo intense self-scrutiny before participating in the Lord's Supper. . . . [He urges people to] examine whether they are engaged in sin and are resolute to forsake it."[2] Failure to do so, he insisted, would invite God's discipline.

What Edwards urged for his congregation was nothing he had not personally practiced. From the time of his conversion, Edwards understood the importance of ongoing self-investigation. Several of Edwards' resolutions reflect his commitment to personal scrutiny, especially numbers 25, 37, 41, 57, and 60. It is necessary to study these resolutions in order to understand Edwards' piety. Moreover, self-examination is critical to our own spiritual growth. Every Christian who reads this book must regularly search his or her own heart.

## EXAMINED CONVERSION

In his twenty-fifth resolution, Edwards sought to counter his doubts about God's love for him. He purposed to probe the depths of his soul to ascertain why he ever would question the love of God. Fundamentally, Edwards wanted to be sure he was truly converted. He wrote:

25. Resolved, to examine carefully, and constantly, what that one thing in me is, which causes me in the least to doubt of the love of God; and to direct all my forces against it.

Edwards desired to be convinced of God's steadfast loyalty, never wavering in his conviction that he had been made the object of the eternal love of the Godhead. He longed for assurance of his salvation. To his dismay, however, he found that he sometimes had doubts about his state before God. So he purposed to examine "that one thing" that caused him uncertainty.

In the first entry in his diary, Edwards made reference to this concern about the validity of his salvation:

Dec. 18, 1722. This day made the 35th Resolution. The reason why I, in the least, question my interest in God's love and favor, is, 1. Because I cannot speak so fully to my experience of that preparatory work, of which divines speak; 2. I do not remember that I experienced regeneration, exactly in those steps, in which divines say it is generally wrought; 3. I do not feel the Christian graces sensibly enough, particularly faith. I fear they are only such hypocritical outside affections, which wicked men may feel, as well as others. They do not seem to be sufficiently inward, full, sincere, entire and hearty. They do not seem so substantial, and so wrought into my very nature, as I could wish. 4. Because I am sometimes guilty of sins of omission and commission. Lately I have doubted, whether I do not transgress in evil speaking. This day, resolved, No.[3]

He returned to this theme of assurance of salvation in a diary entry the next year: "Monday morning, Aug. 12. The chief thing, that now makes me in any measure to question my good estate, is my not having experienced conversion in those particular steps, wherein the people of New England, and anciently the Dissenters of Old England, used to experience it. Wherefore, now resolved, never to leave searching, till I have satisfyingly found out the very bottom and foundation, the real reason, why they used to be converted in those steps."[4]

As these entries reveal, Edwards was concerned that his conversion experience did not fit what he had been taught was the normal pattern. According to Puritan heritage, conversion was "normally an arduous process rather than a single moment,"[5] but Edwards had never experienced a prolonged, pre-conversion agony over sin. As a result, as he admitted in the Dec. 18 diary entry above, he often did not "feel" like a Christian. Consequently, he feared his religious ardor might be only "hypocritical outside affections"—a superficial, non-saving attitude toward Christ that even "wicked men may feel."

About that same time, he wrote the following in his diary:

Friday, May 28. It seems to me, that whether I am now converted or not, I am so settled in the state I am in, that I shall go on in it all my life. But, however settled I may be, yet I will continue to pray to God, not to suffer me to be deceived about it, nor to sleep in an unsafe condition; and every and anon, will call all into question and try myself, using for helps, some of our old divines, that God may have opportunities to answer my prayers, and the spirit of God to show me my error, if I am in one.[6]

By this entry, young Edwards revealed he was not absolutely sure he was converted. But he believed that whatever his spiritual state—"converted or not"—he would remain in it and not revert to his former way of life. However, he would continue to seek certainty about his salvation. First, he would plead with God not to allow him to be deceived about the condition of his soul. Second, he occasionally would "try," or test, himself, that God might show him any error he was making in his understanding of his spiritual condition. He knew he could not afford to be wrong on this most fundamental point—eternity is too long and the lake of fire is too painful.

In short, Edwards' doubts about God's love for him were rooted in suspicions about *his own* love for God. He knew that all true believers love God, so he concluded that if he did not love God supremely, he had reason to question whether he had saving faith. Edwards was at a loss as to why the Puritans had insisted that salvation must always come about by prolonged conviction and violent repentance. Why had he been converted with ease and made to know the sweetness and beauty of God's holiness? Was his experience valid? Such uncertainty about his spiritual state necessitated ongoing self-examination. He was conscious of the apostle Paul's admonition: "Examine yourselves, to see whether you are in the faith. Test yourselves" (2 Cor. 13:5a). Edwards therefore purposed to search within himself in order to discern whether he was truly born again.

## EXPOSED SIN

Edwards further purposed to examine himself in order to uproot indwelling sin so as to cultivate godliness. He was well aware that the weeds of iniquity must be removed if the "pleasant flowers"[7] of holiness are to blossom. Being "truly religious"[8] necessitated a regular audit of his soul to see whether wickedness was to be found. In resolution 37, Edwards wrote:

> 37. Resolved, to inquire every night, as I am going to bed, wherein I have been negligent, what sin I have committed, and wherein I have denied myself: also at the end of every week, month and year. Dec. 22 and 26, 1722.

So passionate was Edwards about living a Christlike life that he purposed to set aside time every night to think about his sin. In this soul exploration, he would consider, first, where he had been "negligent" in his Christian duties. He knew he must not become slack, because any failure to observe a divine command is sin (James 4:17). Second, he would note "what sin I have committed" and promptly confess it (1 John 1:9). Third, he would investigate where he had "denied" himself in daily cross-bearing (Luke 9:23). Growth in personal holiness demanded surveillance in each of these areas.

Edwards also tried to look ahead and anticipate what sins he might be prone to in various situations. He wrote: "Wednesday, Jan. 9, at night. . . . I think it would be advantageous every morning to consider my business and temptations; and what sins I shall be exposed to that day: and to make a resolution how to improve the day, and to avoid those sins."[9]

Edwards was willing to be extremely specific in his self-scrutiny. He wrote in his diary: "Tuesday, Nov. 10. To mark all that I say in conversation, merely to beget in others, a good opinion of myself, and examine it."[10] Edwards fought a desire for others to have "a good opinion" of him. Consequently, he pledged to "mark"—meaning, take careful note of—*everything* he said about himself in conversation that was self-promoting. The way to prevent egotistical words was to examine all such statements and then to repent whenever he discovered self-centered pride in his speech.

He was willing to spend large amounts of time considering his heart. In fact, he purposed to block off entire days for self-examination: "June 11. To set apart days of meditation

145

on particular subjects; as sometimes, to set apart a day for the consideration of the greatness of my sins; at another, to consider the dreadfulness and certainty, of the future misery of ungodly men; at another, the truth and certainty of religion; and so, of the great future things promised and threatened in the Scriptures."[11] As we saw in chapter 7, Edwards was committed to regular meditation on various subjects, and that included his own sin. He understood that his heart was deceitful (Jer. 17:9) and that he had spiritual blind spots. Edwards was committed to investing the time necessary to discover indwelling sin.

## INSPECTED LIFE

Edwards was not content merely to root out sin and live a mediocre Christian life. He wanted to excel in his walk with Christ. Therefore, he set himself to examine his life for ways to improve. He knew that some decisions he would face would be between good and evil. But others would be between good and better. Edwards was eager to reach for the better, advancing beyond what is merely good. To that end, he composed his forty-first resolution:

> 41. Resolved, to ask myself at the end of every day, week, month and year, wherein I could possibly in any respect have done better. Jan. 11, 1723.

In this vow, Edwards purposed to evaluate regularly how he could have carried out his Christian duties in a "better" fashion. This self-examination was to be comprehensive: Edwards wanted to identify ways to improve "in any respect." Could he have prayed more effectively? Could he have studied Scripture more carefully? Could he have used his time more strategically? Could he have confessed his sin more thoroughly? These likely were the kinds of questions Edwards asked himself as he pursued excellence in his Christian life.

In his quest to excel, Edwards resorted to self-examination in order to pinpoint his performance at any given time. As we saw in chapter 5, one standard Edwards used to measure his progress was his own "Resolutions." Edwards wanted to know whether violations of his "Resolutions" were on a downturn or an upswing at any given time. In this plan of action, we see once again his intense desire that his spiritual life should become better. Computing his performance weekly, monthly, and yearly, he sought to stimulate his spiritual growth from one level of maturity to the next.

Edwards also used various chapters of Scripture to measure his performance. He wrote: "Friday morning, Dec. 27. At the end of every month, to examine my behavior, strictly, by some chapter in the New Testament, more especially made up of rules of life. At the end of the year, to examine my behavior by the rules of the New Testament in general, reading many chapters. It would also be convenient, sometime at the end of the year, to read, for this purpose, in the book of Proverbs."[12] By measuring his behavior against chapters of the New Testament that were especially relevant in terms of rules for living, he hoped to discover how he was doing and how he could improve. He also singled out the book of Proverbs as a particularly helpful portion of Scripture for this purpose.

## TESTED DUTIES

Edwards resolved to make self-examination a priority when he faced unpleasant and trying times. He understood that God had given him duties that he must perform, and he wanted to be faithful always. Therefore, he set himself to let his anticipation of difficulties serve as a signal to examine his performance of his duties:

> 57. Resolved, when I fear misfortunes and adversities, to examine whether I have done my duty, and resolve to do it; and let it be just as providence orders it, I will as far as I can, be concerned about nothing but my duty and my sin. June 9 and July 13, 1723.

This resolution seems to indicate that Edwards realized he could become disoriented in the midst of trials, losing sight of his Christian responsibilities. Therefore, he resolved that no trial would distract or deter him from his duties. He determined that when he foresaw trials ahead, he would take stock and then, "let it be as providence orders it." Edwards knew that, ultimately, trials were sent by the all-wise, sovereign God for his sanctification and spiritual good. He simply wanted to remain alert and sober-minded during these challenging times.

Edwards considered the fulfillment of his Christian duty to be of great importance: "Thursday forenoon, Oct. 4, 1723. Have this day fixed and established it, that Christ Jesus has promised me faithfully, that, if I will do what is my duty, and according to the best of my prudence in the matter, that my condition in this world, shall be better for me than any other condition whatever, and more to my welfare, to all eternity."[13]

## MONITORED FEELINGS

In resolution 60, Edwards set up another signal for self-examination. He wrote:

60. Resolved, whenever my feelings begin to appear in the least out of order, when I am conscious of the least uneasiness within, or the least irregularity without, I will then subject myself to the strictest examination. July 4 and 13, 1723.

The warning sign here was Edwards' "feelings." Whenever his emotions were out of kilter "in the least," he purposed to take time to understand the reason for it. He saw that a lack of inner peace should serve as an alarm that something was amiss within him. It might be that some sin, yet undiagnosed, was causing a lack of contentment. It might be that he was failing to trust God, thereby forfeiting his inner joy. These emotion-altering conditions demanded his attention so that he could make any necessary corrections.

## THE SEARCH FOR HOLINESS

In these resolutions, we have discovered that Jonathan Edwards was committed to the strictest self-examination of his Christian life. Such life inspection encompassed a wide range of activities, from searching out the genuineness of his salvation, to discovering inward sin, to pursuing the better over the good, to measuring his attention to his duties. He saw all such self-inspection as spiritually healthy and critical to his personal growth in grace.

The same is true for every believer. Only by regularly scrutinizing ourselves can we engage in the pursuit of personal holiness to the fullest extent. It is critically important that we all look inward, auditing our souls and weighing our motives, as God would make them known. This is the kind of spirituality Edwards sought to experience, and it is that authentic sort that we all must pursue.

I must conclude by asking you: Are you examining your life regularly? Are you testing yourself to learn whether you are in the faith? Are you searching your life for sin? Are you looking for evidences of your spiritual growth? Are you weighing the fulfillment of your duties to God? May you be faithful in your self-examination, looking inward to spur outward growth.

Only an examined life is worth living.

## Notes

1. D. Martyn Lloyd-Jones, "Jonathan Edwards and the Crucial Importance of Revival," *The Puritans: Their Origins and Successors* (Edinburgh: Banner of Truth Trust, 1987), 367.
2. Mark Valeri, "Self-Examination and the Lord's Supper," in Jonathan Edwards, *The Works of Jonathan Edwards, Vol. 17, Sermons and Discourses, 1730–1733*, ed. Mark Valeri (New Haven, Conn.: Yale University Press, 1999), 262.
3. Jonathan Edwards, "Diary," in *The Works of Jonathan Edwards, Vol. 16, Letters and Personal Writings*, ed. George S. Claghorn (New Haven, Conn.: Yale University Press, 1998), 759.
4. Ibid., 779.
5. George Marsden, "Biography," *The Cambridge Companion to Jonathan Edwards*, ed. Stephen J. Stein (Cambridge: Cambridge University Press, 2007), 22.
6. Edwards, "Diary," *Works* (Yale), *Vol. 16*, 788.
7. Edwards, "Personal Narrative," *Works* (Yale), *Vol. 16*, 796.
8. Ibid.
9. Edwards, "Diary," *Works* (Yale), *Vol. 16*, 761–762.
10. Ibid., 787.
11. Ibid., 789.
12. Ibid., 783.
13. Ibid., 781.

# *Soli Deo Gloria*

*In spite of the preoccupation with self that Puritan piety inevitably entailed, Edwards was desperately trying to keep God in the forefront of his consciousness.*[1]

—GEORGE MARSDEN

onathan Edwards lived with one driving passion: *soli Deo gloria*—for the glory of God alone. His master purpose in all things, his overarching aim in all of life, was to bring honor and majesty to the name of God. He desired to exalt the greatness of God with every breath he drew and with every step he took. Every thought, every attitude, every choice, and every undertaking *must* be for the glory of God.

Each of Edwards' seventy resolutions was centered on this supreme passion for God's honor. Through these ambitious purpose statements, Edwards pursued his passion for

153

glorifying God in all things. His God-centered vision pulled him and propelled him forward in all of life.

It was God, majestic and holy in His infinite being, whose sovereignty knows no limits, whose grace knows no bounds, whom Edwards kept constantly before his adoring eyes. It was God, sufficient in Himself and all-sufficient for His people, whom Edwards sought with all his might to please. It was God who became Edwards' goal in daily Christian living and whom he pursued with radical resolve and holy ambition. Amid all his labors as a pastor, Edwards remained riveted upon God, who is the beginning, the middle, and the end of all things, the first cause and last end, and everything in between. God Himself has made the promotion of His glory to be His highest end, and Edwards, likewise, lived for this above all else.

In this day, some three hundred years after Edwards' time, there is a desperate need for a new generation to arise onto the scene of history that will prize and promote the glory of our awesome God. Beholding the soul-capturing vision of this all-supreme, all-sovereign, and all-sufficient God transforms individuals in life-altering ways. This is what we learn from Edwards, and this is what we must experience in our own lives. Our lofty theology, centered on God Himself, must be translated into daily Christian living in practical ways.

May God raise up a growing host in this day that will be consumed with striving to be holy just as He is holy. May God give to His church an army of followers of Christ who are radically surrendered and fully devoted to Him. May such a righteous remnant come in due season for the cause of another Great Awakening. And may Edwards' "Resolutions" be the footprints they follow.

*Soli Deo gloria.*

## Notes

1. George Marsden, *Jonathan Edwards: A Life* (New Haven, Conn./London: Yale University Press, 2003), 50.

# The "Resolutions" of Jonathan Edwards

Being sensible that I am unable to do anything without God's help, I do humbly entreat him by his grace to enable me to keep these Resolutions, so far as they are agreeable to his will, for Christ's sake.

Remember to read over these Resolutions once a week.

1. Resolved, that I will do whatsoever I think to be most to God's glory, and my own good, profit and pleasure, in the whole of my duration, without any consideration of the time, whether now, or never so many myriads of ages hence. Resolved to do whatever I think to be my duty, and most for the good and advantage of mankind in general. Resolved to do this, whatever difficulties I meet with, how many and how great soever.

2. Resolved, to be continually endeavoring to find out some new invention and contrivance to promote the forementioned things.

3. Resolved, if ever I shall fall and grow dull, so as to neglect to keep any part of these Resolutions, to repent of all I can remember, when I come to myself again.

4. Resolved, never to do any manner of thing, whether in soul or body, less or more, but what tends to the glory of God; nor be, nor suffer it, if I can avoid it.

5. Resolved, never to lose one moment of time; but improve it the most profitable way I possibly can.

6. Resolved, to live with all my might, while I do live.

7. Resolved, never to do anything, which I should be afraid to do, if it were the last hour of my life.

8. Resolved, to act, in all respects, both speaking and doing, as if nobody had been so vile as I, and as if I had committed the same sins, or had the same infirmities or failings as others; and that I will let the knowledge of their failings promote nothing but shame in myself, and prove only an occasion of my confessing my own sins and misery to God.

9. Resolved, to think much on all occasions of my own dying, and of the common circumstances which attend death.

10. Resolved, when I feel pain, to think of the pains of martyrdom, and of hell.

11. Resolved, when I think of any theorem in divinity to be solved, immediately to do what I can towards solving it, if circumstances don't hinder.

12. Resolved, if I take delight in it as a gratification of pride, or vanity, or on any such account, immediately to throw it by.

13. Resolved, to be endeavoring to find out fit objects of charity and liberality.

14. Resolved, never to do anything out of revenge.

15. Resolved, never to suffer the least motions of anger to irrational beings.

16. Resolved, never to speak evil of anyone, so that it shall tend to his dishonor, more or less, upon no account except for some real good.

17. Resolved, that I will live so as I shall wish I had done when I come to die.

18. Resolved, to live so at all times, as I think is best in my devout frames, and when I have clearest notions of things of the gospel, and another world.

19. Resolved, never to do anything, which I should be afraid to do, if I expected it would not be above an hour, before I should hear the last trump.

20. Resolved, to maintain the strictest temperance in eating and drinking.

21. Resolved, never to do anything, which if I should see in another, I should count a just occasion to despise him for, or to think any way the more meanly of him.

22. Resolved, to endeavor to obtain for myself as much happiness, in the other world, as I possibly can, with all the power, might, vigor, and vehemence, yea violence, I am capable of, or can bring myself to exert, in any way that can be thought of.

23. Resolved, frequently to take some deliberate action, which seems most unlikely to be done, for the glory of God,

and trace it back to the original intention, designs and ends of it; and if I find it not to be for God's glory, to repute it as a breach of the 4th Resolution.

24. Resolved, whenever I do any conspicuously evil action, to trace it back, till I come to the original cause; and then both carefully endeavor to do so no more, and to fight and pray with all my might against the original of it.

25. Resolved, to examine carefully, and constantly, what that one thing in me is, which causes me in the least to doubt of the love of God; and to direct all my forces against it.

26. Resolved, to cast away such things, as I find do abate my assurance.

27. Resolved, never willfully to omit anything, except the omission be for the glory of God; and frequently to examine my omissions.

28. Resolved, to study the Scriptures so steadily, constantly and frequently, as that I may find, and plainly perceive myself to grow in the knowledge of the same.

29. Resolved, never to count that a prayer, nor to let that pass as a prayer, nor that as a petition of a prayer, which is so made, that I cannot hope that God will answer it; nor that as a confession, which I cannot hope God will accept.

30. Resolved, to strive to my utmost every week to be brought higher in religion, and to a higher exercise of grace, than I was the week before.

31. Resolved, never to say anything at all against anybody, but when it is perfectly agreeable to the highest degree of Christian

honor, and of love to mankind, agreeable to the lowest humility, and sense of my own faults and failings, and agreeable to the Golden Rule; often, when I have said anything against anyone, to bring it to, and try it strictly by the test of this Resolution.

32. Resolved, to be strictly and firmly faithful to my trust, that that in Prov. 20:6, "A faithful man who can find?" may not be partly fulfilled in me.

33. Resolved, always to do what I can towards making, maintaining and establishing peace, when it can be without over-balancing detriment in other respects. Dec. 26, 1722.

34. Resolved, in narrations never to speak anything but the pure and simple verity.

35. Resolved, whenever I so much question whether I have done my duty, as that my quiet and calm is thereby disturbed, to set it down, and also how the question was resolved. Dec. 18, 1722.

36. Resolved, never to speak evil of any, except I have some particular good call for it. Dec. 19, 1722.

37. Resolved, to inquire every night, as I am going to bed, wherein I have been negligent, what sin I have committed, and wherein I have denied myself: also at the end of every week, month and year. Dec. 22 and 26, 1722.

38. Resolved, never to speak anything that is ridiculous, or matter of laughter on the Lord's day. Sabbath evening, Dec. 23, 1722.

39. Resolved, never to do anything that I so much question the lawfulness of, as that I intend, at the same time, to

consider and examine afterwards, whether it be lawful or no: except I as much question the lawfulness of the omission.

40. Resolved, to inquire every night, before I go to bed, whether I have acted in the best way I possibly could, with respect to eating and drinking. Jan. 7, 1723.

41. Resolved, to ask myself at the end of every day, week, month and year, wherein I could possibly in any respect have done better. Jan. 11, 1723.

42. Resolved, frequently to renew the dedication of myself to God, which was made at my baptism; which I solemnly renewed, when I was received into the communion of the church; and which I have solemnly re-made this 12th day of January, 1722–23.

43. Resolved, never henceforward, till I die, to act as if I were anyway my own, but entirely and altogether God's, agreeable to what is to be found in Saturday, Jan. 12. Jan. 12th, 1723.

44. Resolved, that no other end but religion, shall have any influence at all on any of my actions; and that no action shall be, in the least circumstance, any otherwise than the religious end will carry it. Jan. 12, 1723.

45. Resolved, never to allow any pleasure or grief, joy or sorrow, nor any affection at all, nor any degree of affection, nor any circumstance relating to it, but what helps religion. Jan. 12 and 13, 1723.

46. Resolved, never to allow the least measure of any fretting uneasiness at my father or mother. Resolved to suffer

no effects of it, so much as in the least alteration of speech, or motion of my eye: and to be especially careful of it, with respect to any of our family.

47. Resolved, to endeavor to my utmost to deny whatever is not most agreeable to a good, and universally sweet and benevolent, quiet, peaceable, contented, easy, compassionate, generous, humble, meek, modest, submissive, obliging, diligent and industrious, charitable, even, patient, moderate, forgiving, sincere temper; and to do at all times what such a temper would lead me to. Examine strictly every week, whether I have done so. Sabbath morning, May 5, 1723.

48. Resolved, constantly, with the utmost niceness and diligence, and the strictest scrutiny, to be looking into the state of my soul, that I may know whether I have truly an interest in Christ or no; that when I come to die, I may not have any negligence respecting this to repent of. May 26, 1723.

49. Resolved, that this never shall be, if I can help it.

50. Resolved, I will act so as I think I shall judge would have been best, and most prudent, when I come into the future world. July 5, 1723.

51. Resolved, that I will act so, in every respect, as I think I shall wish I had done, if I should at last be damned. July 8, 1723.

52. I frequently hear persons in old age say how they would live, if they were to live their lives over again: resolved, that I will live just so as I can think I shall wish I had done, supposing I live to old age. July 8, 1723.

53. Resolved, to improve every opportunity, when I am in the best and happiest frame of mind, to cast and venture my soul on the Lord Jesus Christ, to trust and confide in him, and consecrate myself wholly to him; that from this I may have assurance of my safety, knowing that I confide in my Redeemer. July 8, 1723.

54. Whenever I hear anything spoken in commendation of any person, if I think it would be praiseworthy in me, resolved to endeavor to imitate it. July 8, 1723.

55. Resolved, to endeavor to my utmost to act as I can think I should do, if I had already seen the happiness of heaven, and hell torments. July 8, 1723.

56. Resolved, never to give over, nor in the least to slacken my fight with my corruptions, however unsuccessful I may be.

57. Resolved, when I fear misfortunes and adversities, to examine whether I have done my duty, and resolve to do it; and let it be just as providence orders it, I will as far as I can, be concerned about nothing but my duty and my sin. June 9 and July 13, 1723.

58. Resolved, not only to refrain from an air of dislike, fretfulness, and anger in conversation, but to exhibit an air of love, cheerfulness and benignity. May 27 and July 13, 1723.

59. Resolved, when I am most conscious of provocations to ill-nature and anger, that I will strive most to feel and act good-naturedly; yea, at such times, to manifest good nature, though I think that in other respects it would be disadvanta-

geous, and so as would be imprudent at other times. May 12, July 11, and July 13.

60. Resolved, whenever my feelings begin to appear in the least out of order, when I am conscious of the least uneasiness within, or the least irregularity without, I will then subject myself to the strictest examination. July 4 and 13, 1723.

61. Resolved, that I will not give way to that listlessness which I find unbends and relaxes my mind from being fully and fixedly set on religion, whatever excuse I may have for it— that what my listlessness inclines me to do, is best to be done, etc. May 21 and July 13, 1723.

62. Resolved, never to do anything but duty; and then according to Eph. 6:6–8, do it willingly and cheerfully "as unto the Lord, and not to man; knowing that whatever good thing any man doth, the same shall he receive of the Lord." June 25 and July 13, 1723.

63. On the supposition, that there never was to be but one individual in the world, at any one time, who was properly a complete Christian, in all respects of a right stamp, having Christianity always shining in its true luster, and appearing excellent and lovely, from whatever part and under whatever character viewed: resolved, to act just as I would do, if I strove with all my might to be that one, who should live in my time. Jan. 14 and July 13, 1723.

64. Resolved, when I find those "groanings which cannot be uttered," of which the Apostle speaks [Romans 8:26], and those "breakings of soul for the longing it hath," of which the

Psalmist speaks, Ps. 119:20, that I will promote them to the utmost of my power, and that I will not be weary of earnestly endeavoring to vent my desires, nor of the repetitions of such earnestness. July 23 and Aug. 10, 1723.

65. Resolved, very much to exercise myself in this all my life long, viz. with the greatest openness I am capable of, to declare my ways to God, and lay open my soul to him: all my sins, temptations, difficulties, sorrows, fears, hopes, desires, and everything, and every circumstance; according to Dr. Manton's 27th sermon on the 119th Psalm. July 26 and Aug. 10, 1723.

66. Resolved, that I will endeavor always to keep a benign aspect, and air of acting and speaking in all places, and in all companies, except it should so happen that duty requires otherwise.

67. Resolved, after afflictions, to inquire, what I am the better for them, what good I have got by them, and what I might have got by them.

68. Resolved, to confess frankly to myself all that which I find in myself, either infirmity or sin; and, if it be what concerns religion, also to confess the whole case to God, and implore needed help. July 23 and Aug. 10, 1723.

69. Resolved, always to do that, which I shall wish I had done when I see others do it. Aug. 11, 1723.

70. Let there be something of benevolence, in all that I speak. Aug. 17, 1723.

# About the Author

Dr. Steven J. Lawson is the senior pastor of Christ Fellowship Baptist Church in Mobile, Alabama, a teaching fellow of Ligonier Ministries, and professor of preaching at The Master's Seminary.

He is a graduate of Texas Tech University (B.B.A.), Dallas Theological Seminary (Th.M.), and Reformed Theological Seminary (D.Min.)

Dr. Lawson is the author of eighteen books, including *The Gospel Focus of Charles Spurgeon* and *The Expository Genius of John Calvin*, both in the Long Line of Godly Men Profiles series from Reformation Trust Publishing, for which he serves as series editor. His other titles include *Pillars of Grace, Foundations of Grace, Famine in the Land*, and a two-volume commentary on the Psalms. His books have been translated into various languages around the world, including Russian, Italian, Portuguese, Spanish, and Indonesian.

He has contributed articles to *Bibliotheca Sacra, The Southern Baptist Journal of Theology, Faith and Mission, Decision magazine, Discipleship Journal*, and *Tabletalk*, among other journals and periodicals.

The focus of Dr. Lawson's ministry is the verse-by-verse exposition of the Bible. His pulpit ministry takes him around the world and to many conferences in the United States, including the annual Ligonier Ministries National Conference in Orlando, Florida, and the Shepherd's Conference at Grace Community Church in Sun Valley, California.

He is president of OnePassion Ministries, which is designed to bring about biblical reformation in the church by providing a clarion call to the standard of expository preaching. He serves on the Board of The Master's Seminary and College and teaches in the doctor of ministry programs at The Master's Seminary and the Ligonier Academy of Biblical and Theological Studies.

Dr. Lawson and his wife, Anne, have three sons and a daughter. They live in Mobile.